Home Education Resource Guide

Fourth Edition

Cheryl Gorder

Home Education Resource Guide (4th edition)
Published by:

BLUE BIRD PUBLISHING
2266 S. Dobson, Suite #275
Mesa AZ 85202
(602) 831-6063
FAX (602) 831-1829
Email: bluebird@bluebird1.com
Web site: http://www.bluebird1.com

Cover by Robin Graphic Designs

Library of Congress Cataloging-in-Publication Data
Gorder, Cheryl, 1952-
     Home education resource guide : a comprehensive guide for
the parent-educator to curriculums, correspondence schools ... / by
Cheryl Gorder. --4th ed.
       p. cm.
     Rev. ed. of: Home education resource guide / by Don Hubbs.
3rd ed. 1993.
     Includes index.
   ISBN 0-933025-48-3
   1. Home schooling--United States--Information services-
-Directories. 2. Teaching--Aids and devices--Catalogs.
3. Educational publishing--United States--Directories.   I. Hubbs,
Don, 1949-   Home education resource guide. II. Title.
LC40.H83 1996
016.649'68--dc20   96-8375
                                                              CIP

Author's Introduction

Home schooling has been growing by leaps and bounds. When I was first home schooling my daughter, back in 1983, there were only about 25,000 home schoolers in this country. Now there are more than one million, and by the year 2000 there will be more than two million home schoolers in the United States.

This is the fourth edition of this book, which has become a home schooling classic and a home schooling bestseller. We have made changes to this edition to better serve the needs of current home schoolers. There is an expanded chapter on educational software because of the explosion of this media. Also note that companies' E-mail and Web sites are listed. There is a new chapter on multicultural educational resources.

We have selected product and services according to their ability to serve the home school population. Some of the companies have been exclusively home school companies from their beginnings in the 1980s, and have developed a fine reputation for helping home schoolers. Others are new to this educational market, but have discovered what a large market it is, and are eager to help home schoolers.

HAPPY HOME SCHOOLING! —*Cheryl Gorder*

FOR UPDATES ON HOME SCHOOLING,
PLEASE VISIT OUR WEB SITE AT
http://www.bluebird1.com

About the Author

Cheryl Gorder has been involved with home schooling since 1983, when she began home schooling her daughter, Sarah. In 1985, Cheryl wrote the book *Home Schools: An Alternative,* which has become a home schooling classic and a bestseller. The book is now in its fourth edition. Cheryl wrote that book because information about home education was hard to find, and she wanted information available to people who were interested. She began home schooling her daughter because of extensive traveling, but soon found that there were other compelling reasons to home school. These ideas became the foundation of the home schooling books she has written.

Sarah thrived with home education. At fifteen, she began college. She has been an "A" student at Arizona State University, and has participated in many extraordinary experiences. She had an internship at the Smithsonian Institution in Washington, D.C., working with world-reknown experts in her field of archaeology. She has studied in Kenya, Africa at the famous Koobi Fora field school conducted by Harvard. She is involved with the Americorps program in Mesa, Arizona, and has been developing educational programs for children. Her current project is writing a book on home schooling.

Cheryl has continued writing and editing books. Her other books include *Green Earth Resource Guide; Multicultural Education Resource Guide; Home Business Resource Guide* and *Homeless: Without Addresses in America*, which won a prestigious Benjamin Franklin award in 1989. She is currently working on curriculums for homeschoolers.

Cheryl is often the guest on radio and TV shows discussing homeschooling, and is available to speak at conventions and seminars.

Table of Contents

Children Educated at Home Don't Become Social Misfits, U of M Study Says

The following article was reprinted from the *Home Educator's Family Times,* published by the Home School Support Network of Michigan, with permission from the University of Michigan, Ann Arbor, Michigan.

Teaching children at home won't make them social misfits, a University of Michigan study suggests.

The detailed study of 53 adults who were taught at home by their parents is one of the first to examine the long-term effects of home schooling—a practice now followed by as many as 300,000 American families.[Editor's Note: As of 1996, that figure is 1.2 million home schoolers in the United States, as estimated by the Home School Legal Defense Association.]

"One of the major arguments against home schooling is that it deprives children of the peer contacts needed for normal social development," says J. Gary Knowles, U-M assistant professor of education. "Public school educators and other critics also question whether home-educated children will be able to become productive, participating members of diverse and democratic society.

"But I found no evidence that these adults were even moderately disadvantaged in either respect. Two-thirds of them were married—the norm for adults their age—and none were unemployed or on any form of welfare assistance.

More than three-quarters felt that being taught at home had actually helped them to interact with people form different levels of society."

For the study, presented recently at an educational conference in New Zealand, Knowles analyzed data from a mail questionnaire, then conducted extensive interviews in person or by telephone with 10 individuals who agreed to the in-depth discussion and were geographically accessible.

The survey respondents were, on average, 32 years old, and nearly three-fourths were women. One respondent was Hispanic, another was Black and the rest were white. "Minority home-educated adults are extremely difficult to locate and identify," Knowles says.

More than 40 percent attended college, and 15 percent of those had completed a graduate degree. Nearly two-thirds of the individuals were self-employed. But only a few worked alone as crafts people or in other solitary occupations, while most either provided employment to others or worked along with family members.

"That so many of those surveyed were self-employed supports the contention that home schooling tends to enhance a person's self-reliance and independence," Knowles says.

"The religious conservatives who operate home schools are strange bedfellows with the often liberal proponents of the practice who support home schooling for its superior pedagogical benefits," he notes. "What both groups share, though, is a feeling that public schools are not serving the best interests of their students, in one way or another. They're perceived as run-down, dirty, dangerous places filled with drugs, weapons, immorality and poor teaching."

Whatever the reasons for being educated at home, the adults Knowles surveyed had many positive things to say about the experience. When asked whether they would want to be educated at home if they had their lives to live over again, 96 percent said, "Yes." They had many warm memories about their home schooling," Knowles says. "Many mentioned the strong relationship it engendered with their parents while others talked about the self-directed curriculum and individualized pace that a flexible program of home schooling permitted. ...This survey and the life history accounts that arose out of it clearly show that, done in an enlightened, broad-minded way, with plenty of flexibility in curriculum and methods, home schooling can be a positive experience for children with benefits that last many years."

Chapter One

LEGAL INFORMATION
ABOUT HOME EDUCATION

State laws and court rulings concerning home education are changing rapidly. The first step parents should make after deciding to home educate their children is to study the laws that apply to home schooling in their state. The most up-to-date information can be obtained by contacting a local home school support group. Many of these are listed in Chapter 12. These groups are parents who are already home schooling their children and they will know how current laws are being applied in their particular state and school district. Many already have a guidebook to help parents fill out forms and to guide them through the legal process for that state.

Alliance for Parental Involvement in Education, Inc., PO Box 59, East Chatham NY 12060-0059. (518) 392-6900. Email: allpie@taconic.net Internet site: http://www.croton.com/allpie/ This is a parent-to-parent grassroots organization which assists people who wish to be involved in their children's education—whether that education takes place in public school, in private school, or at home.

Their book catalog contains various homeschooling and alternative education books, including one that contains information about the laws in New York state, the *Home Education Resource Packet—New York State* by Katharine Houk, $8.

Blue Bird Publishing, 2266 S. Dobson #275, Mesa Az 85202. (602) 831-6063. FAX (602) 831-1829. Email: bluebird @bluebird1.com Internet site: http://www.bluebird1.com *Home Schools: An Alternative* by Cheryl Gorder is a best-selling home schools book that contains important chapters about the legal issues of homeschooling including "Legal Aspects" that examines compulsory attendance laws, competing interests of parents vs. state, constitutionality basis for homeschooling, equivalency battle, and teacher certification issues. 4th edition, $12.95. **See page 176.**

Christian Life Workshops (CLW), Box 2250, Gresham OR 97030. (503) 667-3942. This organization, through their catalog, *Our Family's Favorites*, offers the books *The Right Choice: Home Schooling, Home Schooling and the Law, Constitutional Law Set,* and *The Case for Home Schooling.*

Gazelle Publications, 9853 Jericho Road, Bridgman MI 49106-9742. (616) 465-4004. Toll-free 1-800-650-5076. Email:wadeted@aol.com

Publishers of *The Home School Manual,* by Dr. Ted Wade and 17 others. This book is coming into its 6th edition and is a must for homeschoolers. It takes parents from the very beginning; answering questions about legal aspects, to answering questions about specifics, like how to teach art or social studies. There are many helpful hints on teaching certain subjects, and on homeschooling in general. Especially useful are the appendices, which list everything from textbook publishers to state legal information. Editor's note: This book I keep on my own desk for reference. This book is $24.95. *The Home School Manual,* Electronic Version is 2 diskettes on Windows, $16.

Home School Legal Defense Association, PO Box 159, Paeonian Springs VA 20219. (540) 338-5600. FAX (540) 338-2733. Prepaid legal protection for home educators is provided by the HSLDA for $100 annual membership per family. Their attorneys will personally assist your defense and the organization pays in full all lawyer's fees, expert witness fees, court costs, and all expenses allowed by state law for them to pay. Even if you do not anticipate problems, your membership will help protect home schoolers everywhere. Families who have not yet had a negative contact with the authorities are eligible to apply.

All members receive the bimonthly newsletter *The Home School Court Report*. This newsletter is also available by subscription for $15 per year. Write HSLDA for free brochure and application. Ask for a free copy of your state home school laws.

Books, research summaries and videotapes are available. Research summaries: *Marching to the Beat of Their Own Drum*, $2, is a cumulation and analysis of all current research that has been done on home schools; *Nationwide Study of Home Education,* ($1), is a 1990 study that compared statistical data of home school families and their results with national averages.

National Home Education Research Institute, ATTN: Dr. Brian Ray Western Baptist College 5000 Deer Park Dr.

SE, Salem OR 97301-9392. (503) 375-7019. Email: bray@wbc.edu This organization "serves as a clearinghouse of information for researchers, home educators, attorneys, legislators." Dr. Ray appears as an expert witness in courtroom and legislative testimony concerning home education. There are various ways to join this organization so, please contact the above address.

Parents' Rights, 12571 Northwinds Drive, St. Louis MO 63146. (314) 434-4171. *Parents' Rights*, a quarterly newsletter, is just one of the publications this active group publishes. This group also participates in legal action, hosts educational conferences, provides speakers for conferences and meetings, supports private schools, and is active in many other activities as well. A yearly subscription is $15.00 (price include postage).

Texas Home School Coalition, PO Box 6982, Lubbock TX 79493 (806) 797-4927. They provide information about political and legal matters in Texas. They also publish the newsletter, *The Alert*, which is $15.00 for an annual subscription.

Washington Association of Teaching Christian Homes (WATCH), N. 2904 Dora Road, Spokane WA 99212.	Pamphlet available upon request: *Home School Law in the State of Washington.*

Chapter Two
CORRESPONDENCE COURSES
FULL CURRICULUMS
STUDENT TESTING
CURRICULUM DESIGN

Choosing the right materials for each child is the most technical part of home schooling. Many parents use an eclectic approach, drawing on many sources for their information, and using the child's natural curiosity to guide their areas of study and the depth of study in each area.

Others follow planned curriculums provided by a publisher, a correspondence school or a "satellite school." This chapter lists those who supply planned curriculums, as well as home-based programs, such as correspondence courses. Companies who supply testing and diagnostic services are also listed. Chapter 3 lists textbook and workbook publishers, supplemental suppliers and school supply outlets.

A Beka Book®, PO Box 18000, Pensacola FL 32523-9160. Toll-free 1-800-874-2352. Christian, patriotic, traditional approach in all subjects for preschool through 12th grade. Also available are supplementary materials, teacher's manuals, answer keys, and texts. Curriculum guides outlining the full year's program are available for individual subjects. Write for catalog.

Academic Therapy Publications, Ann Arbor Publishers High Noon Books 20 Commercial Blvd., Novato CA 94949. (415) 883-3314 Toll-free 1-800 422-7249 FAX (415) 883-3720. This company specializes in learning disabled children. They offer tests in many subjects like language, math, reading, spelling, and more. Their extensive curriculum materials are for students from pre-K to secondary adult.

Alpha Omega Publications, 300 N. McKemy Ave, Chandler AZ 85226-2618. (602) 438-2717 Toll-free 1-800-622-3070 FAX (602) 940-8924. Email:aop@home-schooling.com Internet site: http:www.home-schooling.com. This company has an extensive range of products available for homeschoolers. In fact, they produce an 88-page full-color catalog! They offer family resources, home school resources, curriculums, Bible study, home economics, foreign languages, plus art and music education. All materials are written with Christian education in mind.

Their curriculum consists of preschool packages and grades K-12. The curriculum series is called LIFEPACs, and includes 10 LIFEPACS and a complete teacher's guide with all answer keys and teacher helps. Ten LIFEPACs constitute a year's study in one subject. One LIFEPAC usually takes 3-4 weeks to complete. Progress varies according to child's ability. Prices per grade level for all subjects range from about $199 to $299.

Alpha Omega has introduced their new LIFEPAC Gold Curriculum—in full color—for grades 1-9.

Alta Vista Curriculum, 12324 Rd 37, Madera CA 93638. (209) 645-4083. Toll-free 1-800-544-1397. Alta Vista's goal is to provide a Biblical curriculum founded on a Christian world view, directed toward children of all learning styles, and committed to the idea that learning is best achieved through integrating the academic subjects. There are four levels: Level A is Preschool through 1st grade; Level B is 1st-3rd grades; Level C is 4th-6th grades; Level D is 7th-9th grades. Units are $95 each and include student text and worksheets.

American Science and Surplus, 3605 Howard Avenue, Skokie IL 60076. (847) 982-0870. FAX toll-free 1-800-934-0722. Science kits are available, such as *Recreational Chemistry*, a product of the Smithsonian Institution that claims that it is the safest chemistry set made, for ages 10+, $54.95; *Ant Farm*™, $10.95 and *Giant Ant Farm*™, $19.95.

Bob Jones University Press, Greenville SC 29614-0001. Toll-free 1-800-845-5731. FAX toll-free 1-800-524-8398. Free home school brochure, call 1-800-739-8199. This company offers complete curriculum for grades K-12, with abundant helps for the teachers. It is a thoroughly Christian program with high-quality materials. Free catalog—just call toll-free number.

Testing service is also available, using nationally rec-ognized tests which measure achievement and mental abilities. They provide the tests and directions, and provisions are made for the scoring of these tests.

Brigham Young University, Independent Study, 206 Harman Building, PO Box 21514, Provo UT 84602-1514. (801) 378-2868. Toll-free 1-800-298-8792. Brigham Young Independent Study program for high school students has over 160 course offerings, as well as noncredit personal development courses. Some of their offerings include foreign languages such as Mandarin Chinese, Spanish, German, French, and Russian; Physical Education courses; ecology; drug education; contemporary problems; and dating & romance. Their independent study program also includes 300 college level courses, leading to bachelor's degrees. Write or call for free catalog.

Calvert School, 105 Tuscany Road, Baltimore MD 21210. (410) 243-6030. Calvert School has been providing quality correspondence study to over 350,000 students since 1906. It is highly recognized by educators as providing a high caliber alternative educa-

Chapter Two: Curriculums | 15

tion. Grades K-8, includes step-by-step instructions and all materials. French, music and art supplemental courses offered. Advisory teachers available for additional fee. Start any time of the year. Fully accredited, transfer easily to other schools. Newsletter provided to enrolled students. Write or call for free catalog.

Christian Liberty Academy Satellite Schools, 502 W. Euclid Ave, Arlington Heights IL 60004. (847) 259-4444. FAX (847) 259-2941. The Christian Liberty Academy Satellite Schools has over 22,000 students in 50 states and 56 foreign counties. Grades 1-12. They offer flexible plans according to the parents' needs. One plan keeps the administrative records with them. With the other plan, the parents keep the records. Either way, you can select textbooks from 25 different publishers, have basic skill testing, custom designed curriculum, plus materials and guidance.

Christian Life Workshops (CLW), Box 2250, Gresham OR 97030. (503) 667-3942. *How to Create Your Own Unit Study* and *The Christian Home Curriculum Manuals* are just two of the curriculum guides CLW offer through their catalog *Our Family's Favorites*.

Christian Schools International, 3350 East Paris Ave SE, Grand Rapids MI 49512-3054. Toll-free 1-800-635-8288. Christian curriculums for grades K-12.

Clonlara School, 1289 Jewett, Ann Arbor MI 48104. (313) 769-4515. Email: clonlara@delphi.com Internet site: http://web.grfn.org/education/clonlara Clonlara School has a Home Based Education Program that provides families with a comprehensive, innovative program with plenty of choices. Parents receive help in designing and operating an individualized home based education program. Counseling and guidance are always available for enrolled parents. If the parents wish, the school handles inquiries with outside officials. Program serves all ages—early education through secondary.

What's new and exciting at Clonlara? The Clonlara School Compuhigh—a new adventure in individualized learning using the newest in technology and the Internet. The users hook up to the Delphi network for high school courses, and students can post messages to their teachers or other students in the same courses. What a great way to learn!

Common Sense Press, PO Box 5863, Hollywood FL 33083. (305) 962-1930. FAX (305) 964-7644. Their curriculum for language arts through literature for first and second grade is a complete program for $80.

Division of Independent Study, 1510 12th Ave. N., PO Box 5036, State University Station, Fargo ND 58105-5036. (701) 231-6000. Internet site:http://www.uol.com/ndak This department provides independent study courses for middle school and high school leading to a diploma. Courses are now available on the Worldwide Web.

Great Christian Books, 229 South Bridge Street, PO Box 8000, Elkton MD 21922-8000. (410) 392-0930. Toll-free orders 1-800-775-5422. FAX (410) 392-3103. Email: gcb@ssnet.com Internet site: http:www.GreatChristian Books.com Send for special catalog *Homeschool Warehouse*. Satisfaction guaranteed. This is a great one-stop shopping place for homeschooling books of all kinds!

Curriculums available through this catalog are the Little Patriots series, Alpha Omega Lifepacs, A Beka Books, ESP Super Workbooks, Mott Media, National Writing Institute, Penmanship curriculum from Fairfax/ Thoburn Press, foreign language tapes from Teach Me Tapes, Inc., Usborne Books from EDC Publishing and much more.

Hewitt Homeschooling Resources, PO Box 9, Washougal WA 98671-0009. (360) 835-8708. FAX (360) 835-8697. This company offers testing services, enrollment, and unit packages. The basic family registration is $25, and then units are $89 for grades 1-2, $137 for grades 3-8, and $90 per quarter for high school. Each unit includes an individualized curriculum guide, two hours of phone counseling, and a transcript for high school. Special needs package is available. All materials are Christian based.

Holt Associates, 2269 Massachusetts Ave, Cambridge MA 02140. (617) 864-3100. FAX (617) 864-9235.John Holt founded *John Holt's Bookstore*, a catalog through which he sold books about education that he thought were especially good.

Through the catalog, parents have access to materials to help students study for standardized tests, such as the *Comprehensive G.E.D. Program* from Cambridge for studying for the GED, $12.95. **See ad page 136.**

Home Education and Family Services, PO Box 1056, Gray ME 04039. (207) 657-2800. They provide customized home school programs, diplomas, transcripts, and college admissions assistance.

Home Study International, 12501 Old Columbia Pike, Silver Spring MD 20904-6600. (301) 680-6570. FAX (301) 680-6577. Toll-free 1-800-782-GROW (4769). Home Study International is the only preschool through university level homeschool curriculum provider that is state approved from preschool through college. Having 87 years experience, and having been used by over 235,000 people, they are a dependable source. With kindergarten through 8th grade, the options go from buying just the books to buying full-grade packages that include accreditation, daily lesson plans, state approval, teacher services, and transcript services. Kindergarten $210, grades 1-6, $285 per year, grades 7-8, $330 per year. Price per unit of high school varies. This company has an assortment of courses for high school years that lead to state-approved high school diploma. Free course catalog is available.

Inland Empire Home School Center, PO Box 1750, Airway Heights WA 99001. Toll-free 1-800-378-4699. This organization offers student testing, tutorial, and publications.

International Linguistics Corp., 3505 E. Red Bridge Road, Kansas City MO 64137. (816) 765-8855. Toll-free 1-800-237-1830. This company has foreign language programs especially designed for home education that teach Spanish, German, Chinese, Hebrew, French, Japanese, Czech, and Russian. The program teaches you a foreign language by first listening, then reading—the same way you learned English. Ages 7+. Sets of books and cassettes in several levels run $45 to $51 per level. Send for their catalog.

Landmark's Freedom Baptist Curriculum, 2222 E. Hinson Ave., Hinson City FL

33844-4902. FAX (941) 422-0188. Toll-free 1-800-700-LFBC. Total curriculum Pre-K through 12th grade. Baptist orientation. Individualized home school plans. Annual curriculum $225 for first child, each additional student $200. Record-keeping services available.

Leonardo Press, PO Box 1326, Camden ME 04843. Catalog of curriculums and materials. Curriculums include *The Complete How-To Books: 101 Lessons About Language* (Volumes I-IV), which has complete explanations of grammar, syntax, roots, prefixes, suffixes, irregular verbs, pronouns, and other English grammar background. The full set is available for $28.95.

McGuffey Academy International, PO Box 109, Lakemont GA 30552. (706) 782-7709. McGuffey Academy offers Stanford Achievement Testing and Diagnostic Testing, various choices in curriculum (Basic Education, Alpha Omega, etc.), and accreditation. Registration fee is $20, testing fee is $30, and programs run from $250 for kindergarten, to $400 for grades 1-8, and $450 for high school.

Oak Meadow School, PO Box 740, Putney VT 05346. (802) 387-2021. This non-profit organization has created full curriculums for grades K-12. Prices vary for curriculums between $140 and $285 depending on grade and materials. A curriculum overview can be purchased for grades K-12, including titles of supplementary books used in each grade level. This guide is $5.00 plus shipping. **See ad page 21.**

Phoenix Special Programs, 3132 W. Clarendon Ave., Phoenix AZ 85017-4589. (602) 263-5661. Offers junior high and high school correspondence study and high school diploma program, foreign travel/ study, driver education, alternative programs (summer school, remedial classes), science camp, and more. The program of most interest for homeschoolers is the high school diploma program, which is available to students anywhere (you need not be a resident of Arizona). This is a program accredited by the North Central Association of Colleges and Schools. Tuition is $80 per semester course, and students must purchase their own books.

Saxon Publishers, 1320 West Lindsey St., Norman OK 73069. Toll-free ordering 1-800-284-7019. FAX (405) 360-4205. *Saxon Math* series is very popular with home-schoolers. They have full math curriculums for K-12. Each kit provides all the material required: a teachers' manual, student workbooks, and a meeting book (which replaces the bulletin boards used in traditional classrooms). Kits for K-3 are $55 each, for junior high run $44.95-$37.95; and for high school it's divided into topics: 3 levels of algebra, advanced mathematics, calculus and physics.

Shady Grove Church, 1829 W. Shady Grove Church, Grand Prairie TX 75050. (214) 790-0800. This church offers a variety of curriculum counseling, testing and newsletters. Fellowships are available.

Shekinah Curriculum Cellar, 101 Meador Road, Kilgore TX 75662. (903) 643-2760. FAX (903) 643-2796. Catalog of books for Christian home educators: parent helps, reading, language arts, math, science, health, history, geography, art, music, and curriculums by A Beka Books and Alpha Omega.

Summit Christian Academy, DFW Corporate Park, 2100 N. Hwy 360, Suite 503, Grand Prairie TX 75050. Toll-free 1-800-362-9180. Established in 1981, this company offers Alpha Omega *Lifepacs* curriculums for grades 1-12. Choice of 3 diplomas for high school students. Certified by the ACT and SAT college entrance exams. Iowa Basic Skills Test offered in the spring of each year. Two-part diagnostic testing required for grades 3-12 covering 5 subjects. Additional supplemental material and educational games available.

Sycamore Tree, 2179 Meyer Place, Costa Mesa CA 92627. (714) 650-4466 for information about products and services. For ordering, call or FAX toll-free 1-800-779-6750. Internet site: http://www.sycamoretree.com/home.html

Many types of materials are offered by this company, including several different types of curriculum, student testing, and full home school services. The full home school services provide assistance in developing an individualized study program, a quarterly evaluation of the program, records maintenance, free yearly standardized testing, professional guidance by

Chapter Two: Curriculums

phone or mail, a monthly enrichment packet of 50-70 pages, contact with a support group, and even a group insurance plan. If enrolled in this home school program, there is also a 10% discount on all catalog items.

The curriculums offered include the Konos character curriculum; Alpha Omega Lifepacs; ESP materials; and *Learning at Home Parent Guides* by Ann Ward for K-2. All of these are Bible-based curriculum. Testing methods available are CTBS tests, and the Gates-MacGinitie Reading Inventory.

In addition to full curriculums, The Sycamore Tree offers individual materials in their comprehensive 112-page catalog. There's a wide selection of over 3,000 items. There are materials for Bible study, character development, math, grammar, science, social science, arts and crafts, music, cooking and nutrition, games and puzzles, toys, videos and even parent helps. A helpful touch on this catalog is that Bible-based materials are indicated by a special symbol. The catalog is free if you mention this book.

See ad page 50.

University of California Extension, Center for Media and Independent Learning, 2000 Center St., Suite 400, Berkeley CA 94704. (510) 642-8245. FAX (510) 643-9271. Email: cmil@violet.berkeley. edu Internet site: http://www-cmil.unex.berkeley.edu/

This university department offers courses by mail, e-mail, and fax. There are courses for college level and high school level. High school courses are offered in English, languages, math, science, and social studies. Most of the high school courses run about $195 plus textbooks.

University of Missouri Center for Independent Study, 136 Clark Hall, Columbia MO 65211. Toll-free 1-800-609-3727. More than 125 high school courses are offered by this organization. The center is currently developing elementary level programs to meet the needs of homeschoolers. Call toll-free number for more information. **See ad page 21.**

University of Nebraska-Lincoln, Division of Continuing Studies, 269 NCCE, Lincoln NE 68583-9800. (402) 472-4321. FAX (402) 472-1901. Email:unldde@unl.edu Internet site: http://www.

unl.edu Offers independent high school study, a fully accredited diploma program, which means that these credits are fully transferable to local schools, if wished. Home schooled students will need written permission from a local school administrator to enter the program, and a local supervisor must be chosen to administer the program. The program is reasonably priced. Also of considerable interest is the College Independent Study program, for which students of high school age can start earning college credits while studying at home.

Chapter Three
TEXTBOOKS, WORKBOOKS, SUPPLEMENTAL MATERIALS, & SCHOOL SUPPLIES

A Beka Book®, PO Box 18000, Pensacola FL 32523-9160. Toll-free 1-800-874-2352. Christian, patriotic, traditional approach in all subjects for preschool through 12th grade. Also available are supplementary materials, teacher's manuals, answer keys, and texts. Curriculum guides outlining the full year's program are available for individual subjects. Write for catalog.

Alliance for Parental Involvement in Education, Inc., PO Box 59, East Chatham NY 12060-0059. (518) 392-6900. Email: allpie@taconic.net Internet site: http://www.croton.com/allpie/ This is a parent-to-parent grassroots organization which assists people who wish to be involved in their children's education—whether that education takes place in public school, in private school, or at home.

Their book catalog has some books that could be used in home education: *Family Math*, with dozens of activities on measurement, estimation, logical reasoning, geometry, arithmetic, $18; *Kids to the Rescue: First Aid Techniques for Kids* has fourteen illustrated emergency situations, $7.95; *Sharing Nature With Children: The Classic Parents' and Teachers' Nature Awareness Guidebook* is one of this editor's favorites and deserves to be called a classic,

$7.95.

Alpha Omega Publications, 300 N. McKemy Ave, Chandler AZ 85226-2618. (602) 438-2717 Toll-free 1-800-622-3070 FAX (602) 940-8924. Email: aop@home-schooling. com Internet site: http:www. home-schooling.com This company has an extensive range of products available for homeschoolers. In fact, they produce an 88-page full-color catalog! They offer family resources, home school resources, curriculums, Bible study, home economics, foreign languages, plus art and music education. All materials are written with Christian education in mind.

They had some supplementary materials in addition to their basic product, the LIFEPACS. For instance, for geography, they offer a *U.S. Geography Resource Package* for grades 3 to 5, which contains a workbook, a set of four posters, a *States & Capitals* flash card set, and a U.S. map made of reusable vinyl shapes. This package is $20.95, but each piece can be ordered separately.

Supplemental reading resources include *McGuffey's Readers,* a set of 7 for $32, and *McGuffey's Workbooks*: the Primer, First Reader, and Second Reader, each $15.95.

Science resources include an elementary science lab for grades 2 to 8, which has 70 pieces and includes instructions for 150+ experiments, $214.95. This would be something for homeschoolers to purchase as a group.

Backyard Scientist, PO Box 16966, Irvine CA 92713 (714) 551-2392.Email: Backyrdsci @aol.com This company, serving home educators for 16 years, is known for its award-winning hands-on books that teach kids life science, chemistry and physics in a way that makes science come alive. *The Original Backyard Scientist Series:* One through Four and *Exploring Earthworms with Me* ($10.20 each ppd.) are books used successfully by parents and teachers. These books contain hands-on experiments that can be done with materials commonly found in most homes. These books have been named among the top 100 products by the *Curriculum Product News* for contributing to the education of students through superior products.

Written just for home school parents is *Parent Guide to Teaching Science,* grades K-

12 ($24.50 ppd.). Three new science kits are available: *Magical Slime, Magic of Rocks* and *Magical Super Crystals* ($12.50 ea. ppd.). Brochure available.

Bea's Penmanship and Creative Writing Program, PO Box 50284, Billings MT 59105. (406) 259-3050. Email: beas@men.net   Internet site: http://dns.mcn.net:80/~beas/ Aletha McDonald has developed programs for spelling, penmanship, and creative writing. *The Spelling and Penmanship on Student Level* program is for grades 1-9. There's also a *Penmanship and Creative Writing* program.

Bend Cornerstone Books, 62570 Dixon Loop, Bend OR 97701. Toll-free 1-800-487-5952. Free catalog of Bibles, books, tapes and videos for the entire family. They specialize in reprints of literature and historical books.

Blue Bird Publishing, 1713 East Broadway #306, Tempe AZ 85282. (602) 968-4088, (602) 831-6063. FAX (602) 831-1829. The *Dr. Christman's Learn-to-Read Book,* $15.95, is a complete learn-to-read book program for all ages. Based on phonics, this book is widely used by homeschoolers, by teachers, and by adult literacy programs. It's amply illustrated to hold the student's interest. The book starts with the basics, but also includes more advanced material for readers who need a boost in their reading skills. There are stories at the end of each of the basic levels. Phonic rules are clearly explained with numerous examples. **Teachers have called this the best phonics book available! See page 176.**

Bluestocking Press, PO Box 2030, Shingle Springs CA 95682-2030. (916) 621-1123. Toll-free 1-800-959-8586. FAX (916) 642-9222.

Bluestocking Press Resource Guide and Catalog ($3) lists over 1,000 items with a concentration on American history, economics and law. This is an excellent source for supplementary materials in those areas.

Whatever Happened to Penny Candy? 3rd edition, by Richard J. Maybury, is a very popular book that brings economics alive for the student. "Highly recommended."— Mary Pride. "The book is excellent."—*School Library Journal.* Recommended by William Simon, former US Secretary of the Treasury; Dr.

John Murphy, President of the National Schools Committee for Economic Education, and more. For ages 10+, $9.95.

Another one of their very popular titles is *Whatever Happened to Justice* by Richard J. Maybury. In this book, Maybury uses history to explain the difference between a political legal system and a scientific one. Recommended by William E. Simon, former US Secretary of the Treasury; William Snavely, Professor of Economics at George Mason University; many teachers and more. For ages 12+, $14.95.

See ad page ...

Bob Jones University Press, Greenville SC 29614-0001. Toll-free 1-800-845-5731. FAX toll-free 1-800-524-8398. Free home school brochure, call 1-800-739-8199. This company offers complete curriculum for grades K4-12, with abundant helps for the teachers. It is a thoroughly Christian program with high-quality materials. Free catalog—just call toll-free number.

They have a 70-page full-color catalog full of textbooks for Christian schools— *Home School Catalog.* You can order separate units, you do not need to order a full curriculum.

This is especially useful for homeschoolers. For instance, vocabulary is available individually for grades 7-12, each one $6.50.

Bolchazy-Carducci Publishers, 1000 Brown St., Unit 101, Wauconda IL 60084. (847) 526-4344. FAX (847) 526-2867. This company has developed an easy-to-use self-study program that opens the door to a powerful and vital subject—Latin. Study after study has shown Latin is unmatched in improving skills for reading, writing, speaking, spelling and vocabulary. Latin students enhance their skills in two very important functions—communication and comprehension. This program is like having a Latin teacher in your home. Perfect for homeschoolers. Now available on CD-ROM.

Bornstein School of Memory Training, 11693 San Vicente Blvd., Los Angeles CA 90049. (310) 478-2056. Credit card orders toll-free 1-800-468-2058. Memory training expert Arthur Bornstein has devised unique new memory training methods. These are effective learning aids for all ages, and will help children do better in their school work! These products have been designed for math,

states and capitals, vocabulary, and as a whole course, including video courses.

For math, there's the *Multiplication Memorizer System* consisting of 40 flash cards and two cassette tapes, one for the teacher, and one for the student. The tapes explain how visualization techniques bring instant recall and retention of the multiplication tables. The flash cards are extra large, 7" x 11", and each one has a unique colored illustration that helps the child remember that particular multiplication combination. $39.95. There's also an *Addition and Subtraction Memorizer System*, $39.95.

For memorizing states and capitals, Mr. Bornstein has devised flash cards that will stay in the mind of the student. For instance, there is a card with an illustration of a woman in a wedding dress with her arm linked to a big man in a large top hat. This card says, "Virginia married a Rich Man." The association is—Virginia, Richmond. $39.95. Similar system for spelling, $39.95. A vocabulary system is $29.50, includes book and audiotape.

Mr. Bornstein is offering home schoolers special prices on some of his fine products. *The Complete Home*

Study Memory Training Kits is regular price $125; special home school price $95. The *Video Memory Training Course* is regular price $195; special home school price $175. Call or write for free catalog.

Carolina Biological Supply Company, 2700 York Road., Burlington NC 27215-3398. (910) 584-0381. Toll-free 1-800-334-5551. Toll-free FAX 1-800-222-7112. Internet site: http//www.carosci.com

This company has an enormous (over 1,000 color pages!) catalog for science and math supplies. There is an unbelievable selection of everything you can imagine—from skeletons to plant tissues to butterfly displays to microscopes. You name it—they probably have it.

There's some really fun stuff in this catalog—the kind that makes kids go, "Ooooh, ahhhh!" For instance, there's a *Dig-a-Fossil Kit*, which contains a clay block with real fossils to excavate, $25.15. And there's a *Dig-a-Dinosaur Kit* for excavating a scaled-down version of a dinosaur. You can choose any kit for $37.25: Brontosaurus, Stegosaurus, Triceratops, Tyrannosaurus.

They have *Carolina*™

Living Wonders® Habitats, that are totally self-contained—each habitat includes animals, supplies, and instructions for only $19.98. Types: Land Hermit Crab; Painted Lady Butterfly; African Frog Tadpole; Aqua Frog; Fantail Goldfish; American Chameleon.

There's also lots of books on math and science, such as their *Real-World Mathematics through Science Series* for grades 6 to 9. This series helps kids understand math concepts through interesting science explorations. These run $24.95 each, with titles such as: *Investigating Apples; Packaging and the Environment; Measuring Earthquakes*.

Parents with like the series of *Simple Science Experiments with Everyday Materials: General Science*, $13.95; *Weather*, $4.95; *Physics*, $13.95; *Chemistry*, $13.95.

There's many more books, charts, maps, globes, and numerous other supplemental materials available in their catalog.

Children's Small Press Collection, 719 N. Fourth Ave., Ann Arbor MI 48104. (313) 668-8056. Toll-free 1-800-221-8056. Their catalog has hard to find, well-chosen books and music for tots to teens, and also resources for parents, teachers, and family support professionals. The catalog has books in the areas of: creativity, self-sufficiency, science & the environment, self-esteem; fiction, multicultural, history, family structure, parenting, counseling, values, music and foreign language.

Educational ideas: *Good Earth Art: Environmental Art for Kids,* 200 activities including earth paints, homemade crayons, natural berry dye, homemade candles, luminaries, and more, $16.95; *Playmaking: Children Writing & Performing Their Own Plays,* $13.95; many more. Send for catalog.

Christian Family Resources, PO Box 213, Kit Carson CO 80825-0213. (719) 962-3228. Offers science materials such as the human body model kit ($26.95 plus $3 shipping); hands-on science kits with 35 projects ($12.95 plus $3 shipping); microscopes, coloring concepts coloring books for anatomy, biology, marine biology, zoology, more.

Christian Life Workshops (CLW), Box 2250, Gresham OR 97030. (503) 667-3942. Through their catalog, *Our*

Family's Favorites, they have several types of school supplies and materials including *The Learnables* (foreign language kits), Science labs, *English from the Roots Up*, and much more.

Contemporary Books,/ Jamestown Publishers, 2 Prudential Plaza, Suite 1200, 180 North Stetson Ave., Chicago IL 60601-6790. Toll-free orders 1-800-621-1918. Toll-free FAX 1-800-998-3103. Their educational materials include items for reading, writing, math, ESL, and basic skills.

They have a series called *Beyond Basics*, for reading levels 4-12, which helps strengthen comprehension skills, as well as understanding chronological and spatial order, reaching correct conclusions, and identifying cause and effect. Each level is $16.63.

Two useful series are *Reading Drills,* with three levels, and *Vocabulary Drills*, with two levels. These run about $13 each. To introduce children to literature skills, their *Best Short Stories*, available on two levels, covers: plot, character, setting, tone, language, and conclusions. There run about $20 in softcover.

Their math series,

Number Power, comes in nine levels, starting with basic math skills. These run $9.64 each.

Creation's Child, PO Box 3004 #44, Corvallis OR 97339. (541) 758-3413. From their catalog they offer unique time lines like *Simplified World Time Line*, and *Simplified United States Time Line*, and many more. These time lines have some references to chronological events that happened in the *Bible*.

Creative Home Teaching, PO Box 152581, San Diego CA 92105. (619) 263-8633. Catalog of materials for language arts, science, art, music, history, geography, math, critical thinking, foreign language and more.

Critical Thinking Books & Software, PO Box 448, Pacific Grove CA 93950-0448. (408) 393-3288. FAX (408) 393-3277. Toll-free 1-800-458-4849.Email: ctpress@aol.com.

This company has excellent, highly recommended materials for critical thinking activities in the areas of writing, reading, math, U.S. history, science, language skills, and more. For example, in their *Building Thinking Skills®, Primary Book* ($22.95, grades K-2), there are activities to help students understand similarities, differences, sequences, classifications, and analogies. In addition to the book, there are three sets of manipulatives that can be used with this book. In the *Building Thinking Skills® Book 1* ($22.95, grades 2-4) the student builds on the skills from the primary book and also learns about antonyms, deductive reasoning, map skills, Venn diagrams, mental manipulation of two-dimensional objects, and more.

For math, there's *Algebra Magic Tricks* (Volumes 1 and 2, each $14.95), with simple magic number tricks to help students become more curious about algebra.

Cuisenaire Company, 10 Bank St., PO Box 5026, White Plains NY 10602-5026. Customer service toll-free 1-800-237-3142. Orders toll-free 1-800-237-0338. FAX toll-free 1-800-551-RODS. Internet site: http://www.cuisenaire.com.

Cuisenaire rods are almost classics now, as manipulatives for learning math. For those who have not yet been exposed to them, they are colored rods of different lengths used to learn different math skills. The Cuisenaire

---

Company became famous for these. In fact, the term is synonymous with manipulative math materials within the educational field. Now the Cuisenaire Company has grown greatly, and their catalog offers a wide array of products, most of which are materials for learning math and science. There are still the basic rods, but also cubes, colored beads, colored links, plastic colored fruit, sorting trays, sorting boxes, colored shapes, colored chips, colored dominoes, colored tiles, videocassettes, computer software, books, dynamometers (for measuring acceleration), balances, Cuisenaire science kits, and more, more, MORE! Satisfaction guaranteed. Free color catalog.

Cygnet Press, Inc., HC 12, Box 7A, 116 Hwy 28, Anthony NM 88021. (505) 874-3306. *Writing for Success: A Comprehensive Guide to Improved Creative Writing Skills* by Alexandra and Francesca Swann, is a writing program specifically designed for independent study students, suitable for either junior high or senior high, depending on the student's skills, $29.95.

Design-a-Study, 408 Victoria Avenue, Wilmington DE 19804-2124. (302) 998-3889. *Natural Speller* for grades 1-8, which includes graded word lists, activities, rules for spelling and Greek & Latin roots. Spiral binding or 3-hole punched: $22.

Drinking Gourd, PO Box 2557, Redmond WA 98073. This is a *Multicultural Home Education Magazine,* published by Donna Nichols-White, started in 1992. The goal of the publication is to explore and celebrate the diversity of homeschool families. The Drinking Gourd Book Company sells curriculum and resources to homeschool families.

ESP Publishers, Inc., 7163 123rd Circle N., Largo FL 34643. Toll-free 1-800-643-0280. ESP has published some wonderful *Super Yearbooks* for grades kindergarten through sixth. The books are giant workbooks that have been prepared to sequentially teach those basic skills necessary to meet curriculum requirements for each grade. Yes, all the basic curriculum for a whole year of school in one book! I personally used these books and highly recommend them. Each one is only $29.95 and by itself can be the basic curriculum for a whole grade. Books include teacher instructions and are perfect for homeschoolers.

The Elijah Company, Route 2, Box 100-B, Crossville TN 38555. (615) 456-6284. FAX (615) 456-6384. Catalog of materials for homeschoolers for language arts, math, critical thinking skills, science, history, economics, government, art, music and more.

Engine-Uity, Ltd., PO Box 9610, Phoenix AX 85068. (602) 997-7144. FAX (602) 995-0974. Toll-free ordering 1-800-877-8718. They offer teaching materials for K-12. For reading, they offer literature kits for various reading levels. Each Porta-Center Kit is based on a single book. It will help you create a whole language/reading program that uses critical and creative thinking skills. Kit for each title is $3.95. For example kits are available for Caldecott Medal and Honor Books for reading levels 1-3: *Blueberries For Sal; Freight Train; Girl Who Loved Wild Horses; Rumplestiltskin; Where the Wild Things Are*; and more.

Enslow Publishers, Inc., 44 Fadem Road, Box 699, Springfield NJ 07081-0699. (201) 379-8890. FAX (201) 379-7940. Toll-free ordering 1-800-398-2504. Internet site: http://www.enslow.com This company has a *Better Earth Series* that teaches about the environment for ages 11+. Some of the titles in the series are: *Caretakers of the Earth,* with profiles of individuals and activists to inspire students; *The Energy Question*, describes our need for energy and explores the alternative sources; *Saving Endangered Animals;* each $16.15. There's also a series of *Science Experiments for Young People* for ages 9-14, which has titles with experiments to learn about the environment. Their *Science Projects* series for ages 11+ has *Science Projects About Chemistry; Science Projects About Light; Science Projects About the Weather*; and more, each $16.15.

Essential Learning Products Company, 2300 West Fifth Ave, PO Box 2607, Columbus OH 43216-2607. (614) 486-0631. FAX (614) 487-2700. This company is a division of *Highlights for Children,* a very popular children's magazine. The educational resources available are in the lines of basic skills, whole language, building self-esteem, *Primetime Readers*, science, social studies, hidden pictures books, stories from *Highlights*, crafts books, writing skills, and more. Reasonable prices. This series has brought praise from Mary Pride. Request their 16 page full-color catalog.

Eureka, Lawrence Hall of Science, University of California, Berkeley CA 94720-5200. (510) 642-1016. They have been developing innovative educational materials for over 25 years, and now have a 32-page catalog. Examples: *Sky Challenger*, a kit for astronomy that contains instructions and 10" wheels, such as Native American Constellations; Where are the Planets?; Invent Your Own Constellations; and more. This kit is $7.95. *Family Math* is a book that is a math curriculum with activities and information appropriate for families at home, 304 pages, $18.

Front Row Experience, 540 Discovery Bay Blvd., Byron CA 94514-9454. (510) 634-5710. They have a catalog of curriculums, guidebooks and materials for movement education and special education. For physical education, there's *The Physical Side of Learning* by Dr. Leela Zion, helps parents prepare for reading, writing, and math using simple physical activities, 87 pages, $7. Another physical education book is *Funsical Fitness* by Scott Liebler, an illustrated fitness and coordination guide for conducting twenty minute or five minute classes in your home with your children, 175 pages, $16.

George F. Cram Company, Inc., 301 S. LaSalle St., PO Box 426, Indianapolis IN 46206-0426. (317) 635-5564 FAX (317) 635-2720 Toll-free 1-800-227-4199. This company has been map publishers since 1867, so it's understandable that they have an unbelievable selection of maps, globes, and atlases. Besides physical and political maps of the U.S. and the world, they have individual state maps, culture and history maps of American Indians, African Americans, Mexican Americans, and Indians of the Southwest.

They have a Discovery product line for grades K-3 and the Explorer product line for grades 4-12.

They have a special Prime Time Library® with 18

titles @ $1.95 per title (only $32.80 for the whole set, reading level grades 3-6) on social studies, art, science and health, reading and literature, and sports. This is a lot of great reading for one low price! **See ad page 36.**

Great Christian Books, 229 South Bridge Street, PO Box 8000, Elkton MD 21922-8000. (410) 392-0930. Toll-free orders 1-800-775-5422. FAX (410) 392-3103. Email: gcb@ssnet.com Internet site: http:www.GreatChristianBooks. com Send for special catalog *Homeschool Warehouse.* Satisfaction guaranteed. This is a great one-stop shopping place for homeschooling books of all kinds!

Textbooks available include math materials from Creative Teaching Associates, grammar materials from Fairfax Thoburn Press, McGuffey Readers, workbooks, grammar from Isha Enterprises, phonics from Dr. Christman, Backyard Scientist series and much more.

Greenhaven Press, Inc., PO Box 289009, San Diego CA 92198-9009. FAX (619) 485-9549. Toll-free ordering 1-800-231-5163. They have an excellent series called *Opposing Viewpoints*, which is available for grades 4-12. This series has more than 70 volumes, covering nearly every controversial contemporary topic. Each title explores a specific issues with a unique pro/con format. The viewpoints are selected from highly respected sources. Issues explored include: the homeless, endangered species, child abuse, gangs, America's prisons, nuclear proliferation, feminism, abortion, homosexuality, gun control, free speech, and more. The junior (grades 4-9) series runs $11.95 per title, and the regular series (junior high-high school) runs $19.95 per title. There are also discussion pamphlets available to accompany the titles. This series is an excellent resource for thought-provoking discussion on current issues. It's also balanced because it presents both points of view.

HEC Reading Horizons, 3471 South 550 West, Bountiful UT 84010. Toll-free 1-800-333-0059. *Discover Intensive Phonics for Yourself Homeschool Kit* by Char-L. Mary Pride said, " . . . completely non-consumable, reasonably-priced, and absolutely clutter-free program." Easy to teach, easy to learn.

Hands-On Equations, Borenson and Associates, PO Box 3328, Allentown PA 18106. Toll-free 1-800-993-6284. This company offers an innovative hands-on system to teach linear and algebraic equations for students in grades 3 and up. By using game pieces and a hands-on approach, math becomes an interesting game to young students. The system has written as well as video guides. For more information, please write to the above address.

Hands On History, 201 Constance Drive, New Lenox IL 60451. History materials on the first Americans, early explorers, Revolutionary War, Civil War, slavery & the quest for freedom, and World War II. For example, they offer *Freedom Train: The Story of Harriet Tubman* for ages 6-8, $2.95; and *The Complete How-to-Book of Indian Craft* with 68 authentic Indian crafts like leggins, bows & arrows, and baskets, $14.95.

HarperCollins Publishers, Inc., 10 E. 53rd St., New York NY 10022-5299. Toll-free 1-800-331-3761. Major commercial textbook publisher.

Hewitt Homeschooling Resources, PO Box 9, Washougal WA 98671-0009. (360) 835-8708. FAX (360) 835-8697. This company offers testing services, enrollment, and unit packages. In addition, there are supplemental materials available.

For preschoolers, there's Ruth Beechick's *Teaching Preschoolers,* 158 pages, $9.95; *The Instant Curriculum* with 500 developmentally appropriate learning activities, 320 pages, $24.95; and *Math for the Very Young*, using familiar tasks such as doing laundry, going to the store, 210 pages, $19.95.

There's Saxon Math, math manipulatives, Hewitt readers, and more.

Holt Associates, 2269 Massachusetts Ave, Cambridge MA 02140. (617) 864-3100. FAX (617) 864-9235. John Holt founded *John Holt's Bookstore,* a catalog through which he sold books about education that he thought were especially good.

Educational materials are available through the catalog. Some of the materials offered: *Pint-Size Science: Finding Out Fun for You and Your Young Child,* for science activities for children under 8, $8.95;

Material World, a lavish photo journal through the lives of families in 30 countries, $30; *The Math Kit: A 3-Dimensional Tour Through Mathematics,* a fascinating collection of pop-ups, interactive mechanics, pullouts and games for studying arithmetic, geometry, trigonometry, and more, $35. **See ad page 36.**

Holt, Rinehart & Winston, School Division, 1627 Woodland Ave., Austin TX 78741. Orders call toll-free to California office 1-800-222-4658. Major commercial textbook publisher.

Home School Books & Supplies, 104 S. West Ave., Arlington WA 98223. (360) 435-0376. FAX (360) 435-1028. Toll-free orders 1-800-788-1221. Internet site: http://www.thehomeschool.com Free catalog of materials, teaching tools and teaching aids for preschool through high school. They have access to over 400 publishers and 250,000 titles, including:. A Beka Book, Alpha-Omega, Little Patriots, John Saxon Math, Backyard Scientist, Mott-Media, Good Apple, Math Mouse Games, Crossway Books, and more.

Homeschool Marketing Group, Inc., 6226 NE 182nd St., Seattle WA 98155. Toll-free ordering 1-800-481-3466. Distributors of the *America at School® History Curriculum Unit,* which contains 1 teachers guide, 20 activity cards, 2 giant wall posters, 1 set of *American Girls School Stories,* $75. This history curriculum unit shows students how America has changed over the past 225 years by exploring the school experiences of 5 fictional characters from America's past.

Home School Supply House, PO Box 2000, Beaver UT 84713. (801) 438-1254. Free catalog of learning materials.

Home Teachers, PO Box 8724, Stockton CA 95208-0724. They offer *The Easy Reading Kit,* an easy to use kit that teaches phonics. $19.75 plus $2.00 for shipping (California residents add $1.35 tax).

Incentive Publications, 3835 Cleghorn Ave., Nashville TN 37215-2532. (615) 385-2934. FAX (615) 385-2967. Toll-free 1-800-421-2830. This company has a 48-page full-color catalog full of educational materials in the areas of thinking skills, language arts, social awareness, social studies, science, math, and arts & crafts.

Homeschoolers will enjoy the book *If You're Trying to Teach Kids How to Write ... You've Gotta Have This Book* (256 pages, $14.95) that contains specific answers to the questions parents might ask, such as: "Can I really teach someone to write?" "How do I get them to develop their ideas?" "How do I evaluate writing?"

Another interesting title, *Learning to Learn* (240 pages, $16.95) is dedicated to helping students of all ages maximize brain power and strengthen study skills. This book helps improve organizational skills, time management, memory skills, power reading, and more.

In One EAR Publications, 29481 Manzanita Drive, Campo CA 91906-1128. They have foreign language learning materials in Spanish, such as books, tapes, readers, coloring books.

Insect Lore, PO Box 1535, Shafter CA 93623. Toll-free 1-800-LIVE BUG. FAX (805) 746-0334. They have a wonderful catalog full of every possible way for children to learn about insects. There are puzzles, kits, displays, games, videos and books.

For kits, there's the *Human Body Science Kit*, with 21 hands-on activities that give an inside view of the marvelous human body, ages 8+, $9.95; *Erupting Volcano Kit*, just ad vinegar and soda for a simulated lava flow, preschool+, $11.95; and the *Incredible Paper-Making Kit,* recycle newspaper, junk mail and magazines into usable paper in just 30 minutes, $24.95.

Instructional Fair, a division of TS Denison, PO Box 1650, Grand Rapids MI 49501. (616) 363-1290. Toll-free ordering 1-800-443-2976.

They have catalogs of materials for early childhood education and for elementary and middle school.

They have a *Self-Esteem Literature-Based Reading* series, each 80 pages, $9.95, for grades K-1, 1-2, 2-3, 3-4, 4-5. They also have a *Kindergarten Big Book of Everything*, which is really a curriculum in 316 pages.

Interact, 1825 Gillespie Way #101, El Cajon CA 92020. (619) 448-1474. FAX (619) 448-6722. Toll-free orders 1-800-359-0961. This company has numerous catalogs: Elementary; Middle School Social Studies; High School Social Studies; English Catalog (6-12). Their philosophy of learning encompasses interaction and cooperation. Their learning materials are designed, for the most part, for groups, but a few can still be useful in the homeschool setting.

There are some units that are especially interesting to me. "Checkbook: A simulation of money activities in daily life" shows to set up and use a checking account, how to pay housing, food, insurance, clothing, and recreational costs, and how to balance a checkbook. This unit has its own Macintosh software. What a wonderful life skill to teach!

Family Tree for ages 11-18 is an individual learning package focusing on the search for family roots.

Jordan's Knowledge Nook, 2400 Judson Road, Longview TX 75605. (903) 753-8741. Toll-free 1-800-562-5490. FAX (903) 757-6980. They have a 256-page full-color catalog full of educational materials for reading, math, science, social studies, arts & crafts, music, and more. Since they have so much, I'm going to mention a few unusual products that stood out to me. You'll need to see the whole catalog to get a better idea of what's available.

Something I have always believed in is motivational items, and their catalog contains numerous kinds of these. They have award certificates (from $2.49 to $4.95 per package) that build self-esteem & positive attitudes. There's even a colorful Preschool Diploma and a Kindergarten Diploma, especially useful for homeschoolers.

I liked their new social studies series because it included titles such as: *The Three R's: Respect, Rights & Responsibility* ($12.95); *Students Against Violence* ($6.95); and *Rain Forest* ($14.95).

For math, there's *Tactilmat Fraction Pieces* (grade 3-6, $12.95) that contains six sets of fraction pieces representing whole, halves, thirds, fourths, sixths, eighths, plus a frame. Fractions seem to be hard for some students to conceptualize, and this hands-on set will help.

They have *Power of Science™ Kits* for grades 4 to 6, $44.95 each. These kits include more than 40 hands-on activities. The kits are available for electricity, simple machines, light & sound, ecology, rocks & minerals, and weather.

KidsArt, PO Box 274, Mt. Shasta CA 96067. Phone and FAX (916) 926-5076. Email: kidsart@macshasta.com Internet site: http://www. merrymac.com/mspage/ kidsart/kahome.html Free catalog of art teaching materials. Packet of material available to homeschooling groups.

Learn Inc., 113 Gaither Drive, Mt. Laurel NJ 08054. Toll-free 1-800-729-7323. FAX (609) 273-7766. This company offers the program *Speed Learning,* which helps enhance comprehension, memory, self-esteem, and vocabulary. The program consists of 4 audio cassettes and 3 Instruction Guides plus 4 Practice Books for $119.70 plus $8 shipping, but can be purchased in payments.

Leonardo Press, PO Box 1326, Camden ME 04843. Catalog of curriculums and materials for language arts and spelling.

Lifetime Books & Gifts, 3900 Chalet Suzanne Dr., Lake Wales FL 33853. (941) 676-6311. Toll Free for ordering 1-800-377-0390. From their *The Always Incomplete Resource Guide & Catalog,* ($3) they offer a host of quality educational materials.

Li'l Journeys Educational Products, 4600 Morningstar Drive, PO Box 26565, Prescott Valley AZ 86312. Toll-free 1-800-442-7432. Educational products in the areas of: Phonics, art, music, math, spelling, reading, writing, science, history and geography.

The following products are offered: *Self-Checking Drillform for Math,* kids insert a blank piece of paper, do the self test and then check the answers themselves. Available for addition, subtraction, multiplication and division on different levels, $9.95 each; *Alphabet & Number Stamps* are great for motivating kids, comes with clear plastic storage case; *Kitty Kat Sight Words Flash Cards,* Pre-K to Grade 2, each set $5.95. *Language Big Books* to stimulate oral language development. Has suggestion questions and discussion guides. Each $17.95. *Self-Awareness Writing Kits* with open-ended stories to examine dilemmas in which kids might find themselves (cheating on a test, handling a pesky younger sibling) with questions to help the students write the best ending. Set A (Reading level 3.0-

4.5) $39.95. Set B (Reading level 4.5-6.0) $39.95.

Science Activity Centers are kits with illustrated cards that pose questions, supply data and background information, and suggest related experiments and activities. Also contains bonus items such as a magnifying glass, bug viewer, rock and gem specimens, planting sponges, etc. Grades 4+. Comes in *Earth Science, Solar Science, Human Body, Nutrition Box, Plants* or *Insects*. Each $9.95.

Math Teachers Press, 5100 Gamble Drive, Suite 398, Minneapolis MN 55416. (612) 545-6535. Toll-free 1-800-852-6535. They have math materials and manipulatives.

Maupin House Publishing, PO Box 90148 32 SW 42 Street, Gainesville Fl 32607 Phone or FAX (904) 373-5588. Toll-free 1-800-524-0634. From their catalog they offer some unique educational books like, *Caught 'Ya! Grammar with a Giggle, Nurturing Your Child's Natural Literacy* and more.

McGuffey Academy International, PO Box 109, Lakemont GA 30552. (706) 782-7709. The *McGuffey Reading Series*

is very popular with home-schoolers. These books start with a primer and a pictorial primer, then go from first to fourth readers. You can get a boxed set with teacher's guide for $99.95, or order individually.

Michael Olaf Company, "The Montessori Shop" PO Box 1162, Arcata CA 95521. (707) 826-1557 FAX (707) 826-2243. Catalog of toys and games that are educational and contribute to what the company calls "a prepared environment," conducive to learning. The materials are appropriate for learning within the Montessori method, and available for infants to 12 years. Everything carries a full guarantee. $5.00 for a catalog.

Milliken Publishing Company, 1100 Research Blvd., PO Box 21579, St. Louis MO 63132-0579. (314) 991-4220. Toll-free customer service 1-800-325-4136. Toll-free FAX 1-800-538-1319.

Milliken has a catalog of supplementary educational materials for K-12. Home school parents will find useful their *Literature Resource Guides,* $5.95 each, which introduces students to fine literature. Each unit has discussion questions and writing assignments to develop comprehension and evaluation skills. Literature topics that are discussed are theme, setting, characterization, plot, and point of view. Some of the titles for which resource guides are available for grades 5 to 8: *Old Yeller; Island of the Blue Dolphins*; & *A Wrinkle in Time*. Titles for grades 7 to 12: *To Kill a Mockingbird; Fahrenheit 451; Animal Farm; Shane*. For grades 3 to 6: *Charlotte's Web; Sarah, Plain and Tall; Number the Stars;* and more.

Their *Spectrum of Learning* series is also valuable supplemental material for homeschoolers. Each book is $8.95 and contains worksheets on language arts, math, health, science, social studies, and writing. Available for grades K-2.

Milliken has math workbooks for $3.50 each for grades 1 to 6, starting with math readiness, and including time, money, basic math skills, fractions, and more.

Also, for math drills, the *Milliken Math Drill Workbooks*, at $4.50 each, are handy for extra practice problems in math skills. They are available for grades K-8.

The catalog contains many more items of interest to homeschoolers.

Montessori Services, 836 Cleveland Ave., Santa Rosa, CA 95401 (707) 579-3003. FAX (707) 579-1604. A mail-order business that focuses primarily on Montessori classroom needs, and many of the items are appropriate for home education. They feature Family *Pastimes Cooperative Games*, early learning materials, and many books. Some of the most popular items are "practical life" items, things with which children learn to care for themselves and their environment. Examples include child size brooms and mops.

National Teaching Aids Inc., 1845 Highland Ave, New Hyde Park NY 11040. (516) 326-2555. Has 300 low cost teaching aids for life science, biology, health education, and earth science.

New England School Supply, 609 Silver St., PO Box 3004, Agawam MA 01001-8004. (413) 786-9800. FAX toll-free 1-800-272-0101. Customer service toll-free 1-800-628-8608. Parents of young children will love their catalog called *The Book of Early Learning,* with materials for infants, preschool, and kindergarten. There are materials for motor skill development, social development, make-believe, music, arts & crafts, language skills, math, science, social studies, and more.

For motor skills, there's *No Ends Big Builders*, which makes all kinds of structures using brightly colored connectors, $53.95. There are pre-reading materials, such as *Why? Because...* cards that teach cause and effect, $15.95. Wordless books are wonderful for preschoolers, and they have several: *The Three Bears; The City Mouse and the Country Mouse; Jingles, Poems and Rhymes*; each $19.95.

Our Christian Heritage, 7923 West 62nd Way, Arvada CO 80004. (303) 421-0444. Has a variety of Christian influenced textbooks and workbooks in the subjects of history, geography, and government.

Paradigm Company, Box 45161, Boise ID 83711. (208) 322-4440. *Alpha-Phonics: A Primer for Beginning Readers* by Samuel L. Blumenfeld is an effective, step-by-step intensive phonics program for teaching reading to beginners, $32.95 ppd; 2 audio tapes $21 ppd. Now the *Alpha-Phonics*

program is available on CD-ROM for Windows 95 and Macintosh, called *PhonicsTutor*™, $139. There's also a set of readers, called *Little Companion Readers,* to accompany *Alpha-Phonics.* The set includes 10 small readers based on the lessons in the program, $19.95 for the set.

Penton Overseas, Inc., 2470 Impala Drive, Carlsbad CA 92008-7226. (619) 431-0060. Toll-free 1-800-748-5804. FAX (619) 431-8110. This company specializes in foreign language learning tools. Materials are available for ages 5+, and there are books, audios, videos, CD-ROMs, games and more.

PlayFair Toys, PO Box 18210, Boulder CO 80308-8210. Customer Service (303) 440-7229. FAX (303) 440-3393. Toll-free ordering 1-800-824-7255. Their catalog contains great toys, games, and audio-visual materials. Two interesting books are *Science Fair Projects* ($12.98) for selecting, preparing and presenting award-winning science projects and *Math for Every Kid* ($10.98) with ways to make math fun.

Portland State University

Continuing Education Press, PO Box 1394, Portland OR 97207-1394. (503) 725-4846. Offers materials to learn how to improve penmanship by using an italic style handwriting. Course materials are offered for students from kindergarten to adult. Wall charts, desk strips, and other materials are available along with a newsletter.

Providence Project, 14566 NW 110th St., Whitewater KS 67154. (316) 799-2112. CalcuLadder® helps your kids' math skills grow. In both 1989 and 1990, *CalcuLadder®* drills won Mary Pride's Pick of the Crop Award. The workbooks have 192 pages (16 colorful drills, 12 pages per drill), *Instructor's Guide, Achievement Record* and *QuicKey®* grading keys. Levels 1-6 cover basic addition & subtraction through multiplication, division, decimals, fractions, geometric concepts and more. Each level $17.95.

MasterPaks have 48 black and white master copies of drills from 3 workbooks, plus 16 additional drills and all Guides, Keys and Records. Good for larger families with copier. *MasterPaks* 1 & 2, $27.95 each. Samples of these products are available in a Trial Pak for $3 ppd.

Prufrock Press™, PO Box 8813, Waco TX 76714-8813. (817) 756-3337. FAX (817) 756-3339. Toll-free ordering 1-800-998-2208. Toll-free FAX for ordering 1-800-240-0333. Internet site: http://www.purfrock.com

This company has a catalog of creative teaching ideas, including items to help teach gifted students. Some examples of books with activities for children: *Amazing Science Experiments With Everyday Materials*, grades 2-8, with 60 science experiments that can be done in the home, $9.95; *Mathemagic*, grades 2-8, full of math tricks students love, $9.95.

Redleaf Press, 450 N. Syndicate, Suite 5, St. Paul MN 55104-4125. (612) 641-0305. FAX toll-free 1-800-641-0115. Toll-free 1-800-423-8309. They have a 32-page full-color catalog of materials for parents and children, especially early childhood materials. *More Than Counting: Whole-Math Activities for Preschool and Kindergarten* has over 100 ideas for new manipulatives and games that help very young children experience math, $24.95. For even younger children, there's *Responding to Infants: The Infant Activity Manual*, for infants between 6 and 30 months, $19.95; and *Toddler Theme-A-Saurus: The Great Big Book of Toddler Teaching Themes*, with over 60 units of activities, songs, and projects, $21.95.

SRA, Science Research Associates, 70 West Madison, Suite 1400, Chicago IL 60602. (312) 214-7250. Leaders in the development of reading materials and other language art resources. (Editor's note: I absolutely loved these as a kid! Although most of the materials are expensive for home use, they are incredibly effective.) The company has now branched into mathematics, science and social studies as well. Their reading lab is excellent, but one drawback is the price. A suggestion is to share the cost with other homeschoolers.

S.U.A. Phonics Department, 1339 East McMillan Street, Cincinnati, OH 45206. (513) 961-4877. *Professor Phonics Kit* is a simple, but effective instruction in basic phonics for a beginner and special needs learner. Endorsed by Marva Collins, Barbara Morris and others. **See page 48.**

Sacramento Surplus Book Room, 4131 Power Inn Rd Ste D, Sacramento CA 95826 (916) 454-3459. This nonprofit organization offers free literature, reference, geography, math, foreign language, grammar, novels, Braille, science, and many more. 90% of the books are free and some have nominal fees.

Santa Ines Publications, 330 W. Hwy 246 #232, Buellton CA 93427. (805) 688-7862. Vocabulary packets ($7.95, English or Spanish) are available for a long list of books, such as: *A Wrinkle in Time; Island of the Blue Dolphins; Old Yeller; Pippi Longstocking; Ramona Quimby; A Christmas Carol;* and more.

School Supply Room, 3121 Irishtown Road, Gordonville PA 17529. *Right Start Curriculum*, basic subjects K-8. Also reprints of old textbooks send SASE for listing.

School Zone Publishing, 1819 Industrial Drive, PO Box 777, Grand Haven MI 49417. (616) 846-5030. FAX (616) 846-6181. Toll-free 1-800-253-0564. Publishers of over 70 workbooks (plus 6 in Spanish) for preschool through 6th grade. Subjects include grade appropriate reading, handwriting, English, spelling, math, and phonics, $2.25 each. The bestselling *Big Get Ready Books*, a 320-page volume of activities organized by major skill areas, promotes comprehensive learning, 7 grade levels available, $11.99 each.

There are more than 30 *Start to Read* books on sight words ($2.29-$3.95). Also available are flash cards, game cards, and puzzle cards for alphabet, numbers, rhyming words, colors, shapes, math and phonics ($2.59).

Their products are available at supermarkets and drugstores, or directly from the company. Free catalog. **See ad page 48.**

Scott, Foresman & Company, a subsidiary of HarperCollins Publishers Inc., 1900 E. Lake Ave., Glenview IL 60025. (708) 729-3000. Toll-free 1-800-554-4411. Goodyear Books toll-free 1-800-628-4480, ext. 3038. Major commercial textbook publisher. They have a regular K-8 catalog, and a special catalog for Goodyear Books, which are learning resources for teachers and parents. Their regular catalog contains textbooks for reading, language arts, math, science, health, social studies, and foreign languages.

Their *Goodyear Books* catalog contains items such as *D'Nealian® Handwriting* books and math books to motivate special interests, such as *SportsMath Series*, which makes math real for kids interested in sports. The *SportsMath* is available for baseball, football, basketball, and Olympics, $9.95 each, grades 4-8. Another math series is *Stand Up Math,* which has word problems about interesting facts and everyday situations, such as how to measure earthquakes on the Richter scale, how much pizza their money will buy. *Stand Up Math* comes in Levels 1 (grades 3-5), 2 (grades 4-6), and 3 (grades 5+), $9.95 each.

Shekinah Curriculum Cellar, 101 Meador Road, Kilgore TX 75662. (903) 643-2760. FAX (903) 643-2796. Catalog of books for Christian home educators: parent helps, reading, language arts, math, science, health, history, geography, art, music, and curriculums.

Small Ventures, 11023 Watterson Dr., Dallas TX 75228. (214) 681-1728. Materials for phonics, reading, his-

S.U.A. Phonics Department
Professor Phonics

Professor Phonics   *Manual of Instructions*

tory, Latin & Greek, geography, and art appreciation.

Story Time Stories That Rhyme™, PO Box 416, Denver CO 80201-0416. Their *Teaching You Series* has stories of creative arrangement that teach rhyming, nature, math, history, and recycling. Examples: *Teaching You About Sea Shells With Stories That Rhyme, Teaching You About Butterflies With Stories That Rhyme,* etc., each $7.95. They also have educational coloring books with stories that rhyme, such as *Texas Cactus Story Rhyme Coloring Book, Penguins Story Rhyme Coloring Book,* etc., each $6.95.

Straight Edge., Inc., 296 Court St., Brooklyn NY 11231. (718) 643-2794. FAX (718) 403-9582. Toll-free 1-800-READMAT. They produce all kinds of activity and educational mats. For preschoolers, there's *Little Town*, which helps children explore the buildings and streets of a make-believe town, ages 3-5. They have an alphabet mat, a telling time mat, Noah's ark mat, and many more. These need to be ordered in quantities of a dozen, so you can order together with your support group.

Sycamore Tree, 2179 Meyer Place, Costa Mesa CA 92627. (714) 650-4466 for information about products and services. For ordering, call or FAX toll-free 1-800-779-6750. Internet site: http://www.sycamoretree.com/home.html

In addition to full curriculums, The Sycamore Tree offers individual materials in their comprehensive 112-page catalog. There's a wide selection of over 3,000 items. There are materials for Bible study, character development, math, grammar, science, social science, arts and crafts, music, cooking and nutrition, games and puzzles, toys, videos and even parent helps. Complete foreign language courses for French, Spanish and German are available. A helpful touch on this catalog is that Bible-based materials are indicated by a special symbol. The catalog is free if you mention this book.

See ad page 50.

TEACH Services, Donivan Road, Route 1, Box 182, Brushton NY 12916-9738. (518) 358-2125. Toll-free 1-800-367-1844. FAX (518) 358-3028. This company has a catalog of books for homeschoolers and parents.

Thomas Geale Publications, Inc., PO Box 370540, 483 6th St., Montara CA 94037. FAX (415) 728-0918. Toll-free 1-800-554-5457. Lessons for teaching thinking and cognitive skills. *Young Think®* 1 for ages 3-5 is $15, *Young Think®* 2 for ages 4-7 is $25, and *Young Think® Reading* for ages 4-8 is $35. More materials available, up to grade 8.

Timberdoodle Company, E1510 Spencer Lake Road, Shelton WA 98584. (360) 426-0672. Toll-free ordering 1-800-478-0672. FAX (360) 427-5625. Email: mailbag@ timberdoodle.com Internet site: http:/www.timberdoodle. com This company has a catalog specifically designed for homeschoolers. There are a lot of great and interesting materials here—check it out!

They have several types of construction sets, such as a Brio-Mec set, with an engineering curriculum for 4-8 year olds, made of beechwood, plastic axles, wheels, pulleys, and gears (280 pieces, $110). These and the other construction sets they offer provide excellent engineering skills development, and will keep the children challenged for hours at a time!

They also have math manipulatives, art programs, and lots of software and CD-ROMs.

Tobin's Lab, PO Box 6503, Glendale AZ 85312-6503. (602) 843-4265. Toll-free 1-800-522-4776. Internet site: http://www.primenet.com/~tobinlab They have a catalog full of items to help teach science, such as telescopes, science kits, solar engines, balances, binoculars, and more.

TOPS Learning Systems, 10970 S. Mulino Road, Canby OR 97013. FAX (503) 266-5200. This company has developed *Task Cards*, which are designed to let students use trial-and-error to reach a conclusion. This encourages hands-on thinking, and develops a logical process as well. The cards are useful for grades 7-12, and are available for 42 concepts such as: pendulum, graphing, weighing, probability, analysis, oxidation, solutions, kinetic model, heat, and more. Each concept has from 16-36 lessons, and the set of *Task Cards* run from $8 to $16.

Touchphonics Reading Systems, 4900 Birch St., Newport Beach CA 92660. FAX (714) 975-1056. Toll-free 1-800-928-6824. *Touchphonics* is a system that teaches phonic awareness quickly and easily using reading manipulatives. There are four trays of manipulatives, starting with single consonants, and working up to blends, final "e", prefixes, suffixes, and more. This system is easy for both the student and the teacher. You can order a free diagnostic kit to assess your student's phonics strengths and weaknesses.

WFF 'N PROOF Learning Games Associates, 1490-FJ South Blvd., Ann Arbor MI 48104-4699. (313) 665-2269. Educational games that teach logic, science, word structures, geometry, mathematics, set theory, social studies, problem solving, arithmetic and strategy. Equations game for the computer—IBM or Apple. Satisfaction guaranteed. Ask for catalog.

Wildflower Press, 300 Carlsbad Village Dr., Ste. 108A-355, Carlsbad-by-the-Sea CA 92008. Toll-free 1-800-557-5077. Publishers of the program *Getting From A to Z: How to Teach Your Child to Read—Ten Easy Steps!* This is a practical approach to teaching reading with everything needed: flash cards, practice pages, awards, lesson plans, teaching techniques, 2 audio cassette tapes, word lists, and more. $24.95.

Windows to Learning, 8822 Calmada Ave., Whittier CA 90605. (310) 693-3268. FAX (310) 696-9633. Email: wtlearning@aol.com Internet site: http://members.aol.com/wtlearning This company has a catalog of materials available for home schooling, in such areas as handwriting, phonics, reading, spelling, vocabulary, grammar, math, science, history, fine arts, and more.

Chapter Four
EDUCATIONAL TOYS & GAMES

Ampersand Press, 750 Lake St., Port Townsend WA 98368. (360) 379-5187. Toll-free 1-800-624-4263. FAX (360) 379-0324. This company has very fine science and nature games. For example: *The Garden Game*, a board game about gardening for food and fun, $26.95; *The Bug Game*, a matching and memory card game about insects and other backyard creatures, $13.95; *Onto the Desert*, a card game with a poster of desert habitat and instructions that show the beautiful desert ecosystem and its balance of nature, $15.95.

Animal Town, PO Box 485, Healdsburg CA 95448. Toll-free customer service 1-800-445-8642. FAX (707) 837-9737. This family-owned business has been producing a catalog of fine toys for more than

18 years. Their philosophy is to provide toys that promote cooperative and non-competitive play while encouraging playfulness, discovery, and kindness. You'll find plenty to be pleased with in their catalog.

Some of this author's favorites are mentioned, but there are many more. *Everybody Wins* is a book of 393 indoor and outdoor cooperative games—what a great way to get a great variety of these gentle activities on a budget! 146 pages, $10. *Nectar Collector* is a board game that was invented by one of the member's mothers in 1939. The object of the game is to reach the Queen Bee in the center, but along the way, you learn a lot about nature and especially about honeybees. $26. *Dam Builders* is one of their best games. Participants play cooperatively and learn about beavers. $26. *Snowstorm* is a cooperative board game that shows how people have to work hand-in-hand using creative thinking to keep the roads open and get their errands done. $18.

Aristoplay, Ltd., PO Box 7028, Ann Arbor MI 48107. (313) 995-4353. FAX (313) 995-4611. Toll-free customer service 1-800-634-7738. Consider these excellent educational games from *Aristoplay: Where in the World?* for ages 8+ to learn geography, $32; *Made for Trade* takes you on a fantastic voyage through life in colonial America, ages 8+, $21.95; *Hail to the Chief,* for ages 10+ to learn about presidential elections, $24.95; Also available is *Alpha Animals*, an A to Z Classification Game ($24) for ages 8+. This game asks kids to name a mammal or a reptile starting with a certain letter and asks them to name animals at each stop.

Builder Books, PO Box 99, Riverside WA 98849. (509) 826-6021. Toll-free orders 1-800-260-5461. Offers a wide variety of games like *Adventures in Science Kits, Math Learning Wrap-Up Kits* and

Capture the Flag.

Carolina Biological Supply Company, 2700 York Road., Burlington NC 27215-3398. (910) 584-0381. Toll-free 1-800-334-5551. Toll-free FAX 1-800-222-7112. Internet site: http//www.carosci.com

This company has an enormous (over 1,000 color pages!) catalog for science and math supplies. There is an unbelievable selection of everything you can imagine—from skeletons to plant tissues to butterfly displays to microscopes. You name it—they probably have it.

One of their most popular games is the *Food Web Game,* which uses predator/prey interaction among players to introduce basic ecological topics. Ages 12+, $23.95. Another popular science game is *The Cell Game,* which teaches basic cell structure and cell function. High school through college, $31.95.

Endangered Species introduces animal conservation with 20 rare and exotic animals, grades 7+, $20.60. *Space Hop* is a game of the planets, ages 10+, $23.

Pollution is a revised edition of the popular game developed by the Educational Research Council of America. It simulates environmental pollution and the measures needed to control it. Junior high+, $32.70.

There are many additional games and kits for math and science.

Christian Life Workshops (CLW), Box 2250, Gresham OR 97030. (503) 667-3942. Games like Math mouse games, *Geo-Derby*, and *The Backyard Scientist* are just some of the games that can be ordered through their catalog, *Our Family's Favorites.*

Discovery Toys, Inc., 6400 Brisa St., Livermore CA 94550. (510) 606-2600. FAX (510) 447-0626. Toll-free 1-800-426-4777. This company sells carefully selected toys, books, and games of high quality and developmental value. Their products are distributed through nationwide network of 40,000 trained independent Educational Consultants. For a free catalog and referral to a representative in your area, call toll-free 1-800-426-4777.

Essential Learning Products Company, 2300 West Fifth Ave, PO Box 2607, Columbus OH 43216-2607. (614) 486-0631. FAX (614) 487-2700. This company is a division of

Highlights for Children, a very popular children's magazine. Request their 16-page full-color catalog.

An educational product in their catalog is *Best Board Games from Around the World,* with 16 popular board games from around the world, a great multicultural resource, with a short history and playing rules for every game, $16.95.

Great Christian Books, 229 South Bridge Street, PO Box 8000, Elkton MD 21922-8000. (410) 392-0930. Toll-free orders 1-800-775-5422. FAX (410) 392-3103. Email: gcb@ssnet.com Internet site: http:www.GreatChristianBooks.com Send for special catalog *Homeschool Warehouse.* Satisfaction guaranteed. This is a great one-stop shopping place for homeschooling books of all kinds!

Educational games include: materials from Aristoplay, Creative Teaching Associates, Math Mouse games, WFF 'N PROOF games, Bible games, and more.

Hands-On Equations, Borenson and Associates, PO Box 3328, Allentown PA 18106. Toll-free 1-800-993-6284. This innovative system uses game pieces in a "hands-on" learning technique that makes linear and algebraic equations fun for students in grades 3+. For more information or to order, contact the above address.

Hearthsong, 170 Professional Center Drive, Rohnert Park CA 94928-2149. Toll-free 1-800-325-2502. Plenty of interesting educational toys and games in this catalog. Some of my favorites: *Four First Games*, for young children who want to play board games, but are not ready to use numerical dice or count moves; *Mushroom Tiddlywinks* is one of their most popular items; *Cat's Cradle, Owl's Eyes,* a book of 40 string games such as the *Winking Eye*, the *Fish Spear,* and the *Navajo Lightning*; *Parachute Kit* for energetic 7 to 13-year-olds.

Holt Associates, 2269 Massachusetts Ave, Cambridge MA 02140. (617) 864-3100. FAX (617) 864-9235. John Holt is considered the father of modern homeschooling. If you're reading this book, you've no doubt heard much about him. He authored ten books about education including the classic, *How Children Fail.* In 1977 he founded Growing Without Schooling, a magazine dedi-

cated to supporting home educators. He also founded *John Holt's Bookstore*, a catalog through which he sold books about education that he thought were especially good.

Oh Scrud, a spelling card game, $6.95 is available through the catalog. The Secret Door is a cooperative game similar to the classic memory card game *Concentration*, except it deals with the mystery of what's behind the secret door, $15.95. **See ad page 36.**

Jordan's Knowledge Nook, 2400 Judson Road, Longview TX 75605. (903) 753-8741. Toll-free 1-800-562-5490. FAX (903) 757-6980. They have a 256-page full-color catalog full of educational materials for reading, math, science, social studies, arts & crafts, music, and more. Since they have so much, I'm going to mention a few unusual products that stood out to me. You'll need to see the whole catalog to get a better idea of what's available.

There are quite a few games for language arts, such as *Picture Word Bingo,* sets 1, 2, and 3, $9.95 each ages 5+. The game *Language Detective* (grades 4+, $17.95) is excellent proofreading practice in which students look for mistakes in spelling, word usage, capitalization, and punctuation.

Bingo is also available for addition, subtraction, and multiplication, money, and clock skills, $8.99 each. *Dino Math Tracks™* (grade 1+, $19.95) reinforces counting, addition, and subtraction skills.

Smart Shopper (available in two reading levels, $19.95 each) is a game in which students learn to tell fact from opinion—enormously useful in today's world!

For geography, there's *Where is Carmen Sandiego?™* (available for U.S. or world, $21.95 each).

The Learning Edge, 4813 E. Marshall Dr., Vestal NY 13850. (607) 722-6563. They have a catalog of educational toys and games, including felts, *Magicscope*, kid's gardening tools, science kits, Smithsonian games, and more.

Lifetime Books & Gifts, 3900 Chalet Suzanne Dr., Lake Wales FL 33853. (941) 676-6311. Toll Free for ordering 1-800-377-0390. From their *The Always Incomplete Resource Guide & Catalog*, ($3) they offer a host of quality educational materials. They have a few select educational toys and games like old-fashioned paper dolls and coloring books.

Li'l Journeys Educational Products, 4600 Morningstar Drive, PO Box 26565, Prescott Valley AZ 86312. Toll-free 1-800-442-7432. Educational products in the areas of: Phonics, art, music, math, spelling, reading, writing, science, history and geography.

The following products are offered: *Self-Checking Drillform for Math,* in which kids insert a blank piece of paper, do the self test, then check the answers themselves. Available for addition, subtraction, multiplication and division on different levels, $9.95 each; *Alphabet & Number Stamps* are great for motivating kids, comes with clear plastic storage case; *Kitty Kat Sight Words Flash Cards,* Pre-K to Grade 2, each set $5.95. *Language Big Books* to stimulate oral language development. Has suggestion questions and discussion guides. Each $17.95. *Self-Awareness Writing Kits* with open-ended stories to examine dilemmas in which kids might find themselves (cheating on a test, handling a pesky younger sibling) with questions to help the students write the best ending. Set A (Reading level 3.0-4.5) $39.95. Set B (Reading level 4.5-6.0) $39.95.

Science Activity Centers are kits with illustrated cards that pose questions, supply data and background information, and suggest related experiments and activities. Also contains bonus items such as magnifying glass, bug viewer, rock and gem specimens, planting sponges, etc. Grades 4+. Comes in Earth Science, Solar Science, Human Body, Nutrition Box, Plants or Insects. Each $9.95.

Michael Olaf Company, "The Montessori Shop" PO Box 1162, Arcata CA 95521. (707) 826-1557 FAX (707) 826-2243. Catalog of toys and games that are educational and contribute to what the company calls "a prepared environment," conducive to learning. The materials are appropriate for learning within the Montessori method, and available for infants to 12 years. Everything carries a full guarantee. $5.00 for a catalog.

Harvest Time is a cooperative game where everyone participates in planting and harvesting, $15.50. *Sound Track Around the World* is a game produced by UNICEF, and introduces the child to the sights and sounds from around the world, $13.95.

Scientists Card Game

introduces children to the philosophers and scientists of the past and their discoveries, $5.50.

Philications, PO Box 6002-17, Virginia Beach VA 23456. (804) 427-0619. Publishes *Eureka!* (revised edition) which is a compilation of 250 educational games based on everyday items such as cards, coins, dice, dictionaries, maps, pictures, postage stamps, and words. These games are designed to increase the child's comprehension in the fields of writing, reading, spelling, pronunciation, math, geography, history, culture and more. Contains games such as: *Run, Rabbit, Run; Little Magic Cubes; Stampede; A Word to the Wise,* and *North by Northeast.* The book is $40.

School Zone Publishing, 1819 Industrial Drive, PO Box 777, Grand Haven MI 49417. (616) 846-5030. FAX (616) 846-6181. Toll-free 1-800-253-0564. *Games and Fun Packs* (multiple games in one) for alphabet, numbers, map reading, animals and habitats, dominoes, and bingo ($6.99-$14.99). Free catalog.

See ad page 48.

Sycamore Tree, 2179 Meyer

Place, Costa Mesa CA 92627. (714) 650-4466 for information about products and services. For ordering, call or FAX toll-free 1-800-779-6750. Internet site: http://www.sycamoretree.com/home.html

In addition to full curriculums, The Sycamore Tree offers individual materials in their comprehensive 112-page catalog. There's a wide selection of over 3,000 items. The catalog is free if you mention this book.

Toys offered include: *Erector Sets and Bibleopoly,* a game played like *Monopoly®* but based on the Bible. Klutz products are also available, such as: *Braids and Bows,* a kit with a book and accessories on how to make fancy hairdos; *Explorabook,* which is a children's museum in a book with accessories such as a mirror, a moiré spinner, and much more; *Klutz Classic Board Games,* with 15 classic board games and all accessories in one kit.

The most popular book on games is *Cat's Cradle, Owl's Eye: A Book of String Games,* with string games and figures from around the world; highly illustrated.

See ad page 50.

Timberdoodle Company, E1510 Spencer Lake Road, Shelton WA 98584. (360) 426-0672. Toll-free ordering 1-800-478-0672. FAX (360) 427-5625. Email: mailbag@timberdoodle.com Internet site:http:www.timberdoodle.com This company has a catalog specifically designed for homeschoolers. There's a lot of great and interesting materials here—check it out!

Science games in their catalog include *Science Start* ($15) for ages 5-8 and *Nature Start* ($12) for ages 6-9, each packed with experiments for a hands-on adventure. Another good science game is *Onto the Desert* ($11.50) which teaches about the delicate but beautiful desert ecology.

WFF 'N PROOF Learning Games Associates, 1490-FJ South Blvd., Ann Arbor MI 48104-4699. (313) 665-2269. Educational games that teach logic, science, word structures, geometry, mathematics, set theory, social studies, problem solving, arithmetic and strategy. Equations game for the computer—IBM or Apple. Satisfaction guaranteed. Ask for catalog.

Chapter Five

EDUCATIONAL SOFTWARE

This chapter lists educational software, such as CD-ROMs, and also includes courses that are available on the Internet, another new development that's appealing to homeschoolers.

In the directory, each company's Web site is listed. Check these for valuable information. Also, there's *Homeschool Guide to the Online World,* with updates on homeschool web sites. Find this at: http://www.ssnet.com/~hsguide/online.html

Abbott Computer Training, Inc., PO Box 77527, Steamboat Springs CO 80477 (970) 870-6673. This company has written a manual, *English Composition and Word Processing with Student Writing Center*™, that is an instructional companion to the software, *Student Writing Center*™. This 300-page book ($29.95) is easy to follow, self-paced, and includes an introduction to Windows™, wordprocessing, sentence and paragraph construction, daily journal writing, and more. **See ad page 75.**

Alpha Omega Publications, 300 N. McKemy Ave, Chandler AZ 85226-2618. (602) 438-2717 Toll-free 1-800-622-3070 FAX (602) 940-8924. Email: aop@home-schooling. com Internet site: http:// www.home-schooling.com. This company has an extensive range of products available for homeschoolers. In fact, they produce an 88-page full-color catalog! All materials are written with Christian education in mind.

New in this catalog is Christian education software. For preschoolers there's *Rev-Up™* for *Reading, Rev-Up™ for Writing*, and *Rev-Up™ for Arithmetic.* The programs contain charming, animated characters from the *Amazing Bible* video series, and use traditional teaching methods coupled with advanced CD-ROM technology. Available on CD-ROM for windows, $14.95 each.

Bible Builder and Captain Bible teaches Bible skills with colorful, animated scenes and different skill levels. This was the winner of the 1993 "Reader's Choice Award" by *Christian Computing Magazine.* CD-ROM for IBM, $14.95 each.

ArsNova, Box 637, Kirkland WA 98083-0637. (206) 828-2711. FAX (206) 889-0359. Toll-free 1-800-445-4866. *Practica Musica™* gives ear training and music theory, from beginning to advanced, using sounds from piano, guitar, organ, and voice. This is appropriate for high school and college level, available for any Macintosh since MacPlus, including Power Macintosh, us-ing System 6 or System 7, $140.

For younger children, there's *A Little Kidmusic™*, which is for kids 3-13, teaches music notation, pitches, how to play a tune, rhythm with sounds of piano, guitar, organ, and voices. Available for any Macintosh using System 6, $75.

Bob Jones University Press, Greenville SC 29614-0001. Toll-free 1-800-845-5731. FAX toll-free 1-800-524-8398. Free home school brochure, call 1-800-739-8199. Educational computer programs for independent or directed use. All programs have been screened for educational worth, compatibility with Christian philosophy, and cost-effectiveness. Examples of their software: *Mavis Beacon Teaches Typing,* grades 7-12, $49.95*; ASK it,* grades 4-12, a test-generation software, IBM or Macintosh, $49.95. Free brochure—just call toll-free number.

Bolchazy-Carducci Publishers, 1000 Brown St., Unit 101, Wauconda IL 60084. (847) 526-4344. FAX (847) 526-2867. This company has developed an easy-to-use self-study program that opens the door to a powerful and vital subject—Latin. Study after study has shown Latin is unmatched in improving skills for reading, writing, speaking, spelling and vocabulary. Latin students enhance their skills in two very important functions—communication and comprehension. This program is like having a Latin teacher in your home! Perfect for homeschoolers. Now available on CD-ROM.

Broderbund Software, PO Box 6144, Novato CA 94948-6144. (415) 382-4400. This company has educational software that is available at your local software store.

One of their most popular titles has been *Where in the World is Carmen Sandiego?* This software turns world geography into a thrilling chase for kids ages 9+.

They also have *Sheila Rae, the Brave,* which as won over 60 awards. It contains 20 interactive pages and helps kids ages 3 to 7 with word recognition, vocabulary, and spatial reasoning.

Their *ABC by Dr. Seuss* is one of their *Living Books,* which are children's books and literature brought to life. The child can click on a word or an object to get more information.

Carolina Biological Supply Company, 2700 York Road., Burlington NC 27215-3398. (910) 584-0381. Toll-free 1-800-334-5551. Toll-free FAX 1-800-222-7112. Internet site: http//www.carosci.com

This company has an enormous (over 1,000 color pages!) catalog for science and math supplies. There is an unbelievable selection of everything you can imagine—from skeletons to plant tissues to butterfly displays to microscopes. You name it—they probably have it.

There are 30 pages in the catalog devoted to science and math software, so there's a very large selection. For elementary science, grades 4 to 9, they have software titles ($60 each) on CD-ROM for Macintosh or IBM called: *Elementary Science: The Oceans; Elementary Science: The Universe; Elementary Science: The Earth;* and of course, *Elementary Science.*

For junior high to high school, there's a *Marine Life Series* ($59.95 each) that teaches anatomy, biological function, and vocabulary. Titles in the series are: *Marine Invertebrates; Anatomy of a Fish; Sea Lamprey; Anatomy of a Shark.* Available for Macintosh or IBM.

Their CD-ROM multimedia series is appropriate for junior high to college and available for Macintosh or IBM. This series is available on such topics as: *The Five Kingdoms of Life; Cell Biology; Basic Genetics; Heredity; Evolution; Ecosystems; Biomes; Introduction to Vertebrates; Basic Plant Anatomy;* and *Basic Botany.*

There's much more available in areas of math, chemistry, nuclear, electricity, ecology, genetics, anatomy, space science, weather, and more.

Clonlara School, 1289 Jewett, Ann Arbor MI 48104. (313) 769-4515. Email: clonlara@delphi.com Internet site: http://web.grfn.org/education/clonlara

What's new and exciting at Clonlara? The Clonlara School Compuhigh—a new adventure in individualized learning using the newest in technology and the Internet. The users hook up to the Delphi network for high school courses, and students can post messages to their teachers or other students in the same courses. What a great way to learn!

Compuserve, 5000 Arlington Centre Blvd., Columbus OH 43220. Compuserve now has parental-control software, which help parents block objectionable sites on Compuserve and on the Internet. To find out more, visit the Tip Sheet Web site at http://www.compuserve.com/index/tipsheet.html

Critical Thinking Books & Software, PO Box 448, Pacific Grove CA 93950-0448. (408) 393-3288. FAX (408) 393-3277. Toll-free 1-800-458-4849.Email: ctpress@aol.com.

This company has excellent, highly recommended materials for critical thinking activities in the areas of writing, reading, math, U.S. history, science, language skills, and more. *Memory Challenge! Software* (grades K-adult) has several easy-to-use activities to strengthen visual-memory skills. Available for DOS, Windows or Macintosh, $60. *What's My Logic Software* (grades 3-adult) has mind-stretching figural and verbal games to enhance reasoning skills. Available for Apple, Windows or Macintosh, $65. For math, there's *Five in a Row Mental Math Software* (grades 2-adult), with activities to exercise critical thinking skill by combining problem

---

solving with fundamental math operations. Available for Windows or Macintosh, $65.

Cuisenaire Company, 10 Bank St., White Plains NY 10606-5026. Toll-free 1-800-237-3142. Cuisenaire rods are almost classics now, as manipulatives for learning math. Now the Cuisenaire Company has grown greatly, and their catalog offers a wide array of products, most of which are materials for learning math and science.

Their catalog includes educational math computer software, such as *Unifix Software*™: *Access to Math*. This software is designed for preschool and early elementary grades and allows many children with special needs to access math manipulatives. Menus are in English and Spanish. Requires Macintosh System 7.0 or later, 3 mg RAM, $79.95.

Another software is *Building Perspective*, which was Winner of the Best Software of the Year by *Classroom Computer Learning*. This is a computer game of spatial perception, and student work with an array of buildings to predict how it will appear from above. They gather information, look for patterns, and make projec-

tions. Available for Apple, Macintosh, and Windows at $79 each.

James Discovers Math™ is an interactive introduction to math with 10 activity areas. Includes a 40-piece set of Attrilinks and a teacher's guide with lesson plans and ideas. Available for Windows, $69.95. Satisfaction guaranteed. Free color catalog.

Davda Corporation, 7074 N. Western Ave., Chicago IL 60645. (312) 465-4070 FAX (312) 262-9298 Internet site: http://www.davka.com

Davda Corporation presents the best in Judaic software. Children will love *Noah and the Rainbow*, an animated book on CD-ROM which encourages reading comprehension skills. This CD-ROM is $44.95 and requires sound card and speakers.

Davidson and Associates, Inc., PO Box 2961, Torrance CA 90509. Customer service toll-free 1-800-545-7677. FAX (310) 793-0603. Internet site: http://www.davd.com. This company has a full-color 48-page catalog of educational software called *The Educational Advantage*. In it are software for writing, language arts, reading, math, history, typing, science, ESL, early learning, and more. There are items for Macintosh or Windows, and the catalog lists all system requirements for each software. Many of these products are available in your local software stores.

For early learning, there's a line of Davidson/Fisher-Price products: *Ready for School*™ ($79.95) with alphabet and letter recognition, numbers and counting, sorting and matching; *ABC's Featuring the Jungle Jukebox*™ ($49.95) where the students will learn the alphabet while singing along; *1-2-3's Featuring the Counting Critters*™ ($49.95) that teaches kids their numbers as students ride the bus to the bakery, to the concert hall, and to the post office; and more.

For math, there's the popular *Math Blaster 1*™ and *Math Blaster Jr.*™ (each $79.95). The original Math Blaster won numerous awards, including Editors Choice from *Newsweek*, Software Pick from *Parents Magazine*, and a Parents' Choice Award. Needless to say, this is excellent software that kids love and they learn math interactively.

In a similar vein, there's *Reading Blaster*™ ($79.95) and *Reading Blaster Jr.*™ ($59.95) with phonics lessons and vocabulary drills.

For early readers (Pre-K to grade 3), there's *Magic Tales*™ (each $59.95) with stories that magically come to life: *Baba Yaga and the Magic Geese*™: *A Russian Folk Tale; Imo and the King*™: *An African Folk Tale; The Little Samurai*™: *A Japanese Folk Tale.*

They also sell products by Dinosoft™ and other software companies, so be sure to check out this catalog of wonderful software.

Edmark, 6727 185th Ave NE, PO Box 97021, Redmond WA 98073-9721. (206) 556-8400. FAX (206) 556-8430. Toll-free ordering 1-800-362-2890. Customer Service Email: edmarkteam@edmark.com Internet site: http://www.edmark.com They have educational software for preschool through 8th grades. For preschoolers, there's *Sammy's Science House,* which has 5 activities to build early science skills. *Baily's Book House* for preschool through 2nd grade, helps young people learn letters, words, rhyming and storytelling with 5 activities. One of the activities lets kids create and print cards. Both of these are available for Macintosh or Windows, $59.95.

For older kids, there's: *Destination: Rain Forest*, filled with the lush sights and sounds of the rain forest, that teaches ecology and wildlife facts; *Destination: Pyramids,* which helps students experience the mystery of ancient Egypt as they create books featuring pyramids, hieroglyphs, pharaohs, and mummies. The *Destination* series is available on a CD-ROM that works on Macintosh or Windows, $39.95.

George F. Cram Company, Inc., 301 S. LaSalle St., PO Box 426, Indianapolis IN 46206-0426. (317) 635-5564 FAX (317) 635-2720 Toll-free 1-800-227-4199. This company has been a map publisher since 1867, so it's understandable that they have an unbelievable selection of maps, globes, and atlases.

They have a set of books called *Grandfather's Stories*. Each book is $6.95 (and whole series is available on CD-ROM for $69.95). There are *Grandfather's Stories from Germany, Grandfather's Stories from Cambodia, Grandfather's Sto-ries from the Philippines, Grandfather's Stories from Viet Nam,* and *Grandfather's Sto-ries from Mexico. Booklist* said that these books are "a useful addition to any collection."

Other CD-ROMs available are *Atlas of U.S. Presidents* (Macintosh or IBM, $50) with personal facts, biographies, speeches, illustrations, and profiles of the First Ladies; *Crosscountry U.S.A.* that is an interactive simulation of driving a truck across the country (Macintosh or IBM, $99); and *Return to the Moon,* where the user can use a flight simulator, learn spacecraft design, and view past lunar explorations, $45.

There's a series of CD-ROMs for world history: *The Road to Ancient Egypt, The Road to Ancient Greece*, and *The Road to Ancient Rome.* Each program looks at the culture, its rise and fall, its art, philosophy, architecture, and lifestyle. Each CD-ROM for either Macintosh or PC is $134, or $334 for set of 3. This series is also available on video. **See ad page 36.**

Great Christian Books, 229 South Bridge Street, PO Box 8000, Elkton MD 21922-8000. (410) 392-0930. Toll-free orders 1-800-775-5422.

FAX (410) 392-3103. Email: gcb@ssnet.com Internet site: http:www.GreatChristianBooks.com Send for special catalog *Homeschool Warehouse.* Satisfaction guaranteed. This is a great one-stop shopping place for homeschooling books of all kinds!

There's now a *Homeschool Guide to The Online World*, $9.95, also information at Internet site: http://www.ssnet.com/~hsguide/online.html

There's also *GeoSafari,* which comes with a game unit ($84.95), then you buy card packs ($14.95 each) to use on it. This has been a popular way for kids to learn geography.

HEC Reading Horizons, 3471 South 550 West, Bountiful UT 84010. Toll-free 1-800-333-0059. *Discover Intensive Phonics for Yourself Computer Courseware for Windows* by Char-L. Mary Pride said, "...completely non-consumable, reasonably-priced, and absolutely clutter-free program." Easy to teach, easy to learn.

Learning Company, 6493 Kaiser Drive, Fremont CA 94555. Toll-free 1-800-852-2255. This company has a catalog of educational software for reading, writing, spelling, math, foreign language, and more.

One good item for homeschoolers is *Score Builder for the SAT,* which will help college bound students increase their achievement test scores. Available on CD-ROM for either Macintosh or Windows, $60.

The company has software for learning Spanish, German, French, (CD-ROM for Macintosh or Windows, $109 each) and Japanese (CD-ROM Macintosh $60), as well as vocabulary builders for these languages.

For early learners, ages 3-6, they have *Interactive Reading Journey*™ (CD-ROM Macintosh or Windows, $99) which helps children learn to read with 40 storybooks, over 100 phonics lessons, and 20 different lands to explore.

Reading Development Library™ (CD-ROM for Macintosh or Windows, $50) is available in Level 1 and Level 2. Level 1 has *The Three Little Pigs* and *Goldilocks and the Three Bears*; Level 2 has *Jack and the Beanstalk* and *City Mouse, Country Mouse.* Each book is targeted to a specific reading development, using vocabulary that will give children reading success and build their confidence.

There's more available in their catalog. For retailers near you, or for their catalog, call 1-800-852-2255.

M&M Software, PO Box 15769, Long Beach CA 90815. (310) 420-2655. FAX (310) 420-2955. Toll-free 1-800-642-6163.Email: mmsoft @aol.com Catalog of educational public domain and shareware software with nothing over $4.95.

MacSoft, The WizardWorks Group, 3850 Annapolis Lane, Ste 100, Minneapolis MN 55447-5443. (612) 559-5301. Toll-free 1-800-229-2714. FAX (612) 577-0631. Most of this company's software is game-oriented, (such as chess, video poker, etc.), but there are a couple of products that I do like for kids. One is *Match Race*, which helps kids develop their concentration skills and practice letter identification. The other is *Numbers & Counting*, which has 7 games to help kids learn about numbers. Either software works with Macintosh with color monitor running System 6 or higher, $14.99 each.

Meridian Creative Group, 5178 Station Road, Erie PA 16510-4636. (814) 898-2612. Toll-free 1-800-695-9427. FAX (814) 898-0683. Internet site: www.meridiancg.com

This company has developed several technology-based supplemental programs which are designed to be user-friendly tutorials—and they are fun to use!

Their most popular program is *Oval Office: Challenge of the Presidency,* which is a gold award winner in the educational category for the 1996 NewMedia Invision Award. This program is designed for ages 10+, and gives the user a first-hand experience in the office of the President of the U.S. As President, the user nominates candidates to the Supreme Court, proposes a budget to Congress, conducts a press conference, signs legislation, runs for re-election, and learns what the process is all about. Available for both Macintosh and IBM CD-ROM versions, $49.95.

Rookie Reporter "On the Beat" for ages 9 to 14, is another interesting software. The user takes a tour through a newspaper facility, goes "on the beat" to get "the scoop" and publishes a newsletter. Macintosh and IBM CD-ROM versions, $59.95.

They also have math and safety software.

Milliken Publishing Company, 1100 Research Blvd., PO Box 21579, St. Louis MO 63132-0579. (314) 991-4220. Toll-free customer service 1-800-325-4136. Toll-free FAX 1-800-538-1319.

Milliken has a catalog of software for home and school. They have a series called *Math Mastery* for Macintosh, MS-DOS, and Apple II, for only $19.95 each. The series comes in the titles: *Number Readiness; Addition; Subtraction; Division; Multiplication; Integers; Fractions; Decimals; Percents*; and more. This series also comes on one CD-ROM.

Milliken Research Writer is a valuable resource for research paper writing. Students are systematically guided through their thinking, research, and writing with 50 activities. Ages 8+, CD-ROM for Macintosh or Windows, $34.95.

For ages 3 to 8, there's *Marvin the Moose*, volumes I to IV, which teaches moral values. This is a read-aloud adventure that approaches subjects such as peer pressure, handicaps, and teamwork. Activity disk included. Each volume

$29.95, for Windows and Macintosh CD-ROM.

Mindscape, 88 Rowland Way, Novato CA 94945. Toll-free ordering 1-800-231-3088. FAX (415) 897-9956. Mindscape has a full-color catalog of educational software for early learning, creativity, geography, problem-solving, typing, and more.

One popular software title of theirs is *Mavis Beacon Teaching Typing*™ ($59.95) and *Mavis Beacon Teaching Typing*™ *for Kids* ($49.95), which is probably the bestselling typing software available. There are interactive games that will teach keyboard mastery. Available for Macintosh, Windows, and on CD-ROM.

When I purchased my new Macintosh Power PC, there was free software in the package. One was Mindscape's *The San Diego Zoo*™ *presents ... The Animals!*® ($49.95) It was my first adventure with multimedia CD-ROM software, and boy, is it fun! You can travel around the San Diego Zoo on this software, hearing the tropical jungle sounds, seeing the colorful displays, and learn about zoology, geography, and biological sciences.

Another one of their interesting products is *Secrets of the Pyramids* ($39.95), which is a problem-solving software. Kids go on a guided tour of the famous Egyptian pyramids, and are able to play a challenging adventure game. I've always recommended that children learn problem-solving skills through fun activities, and this fits that category.

Check their catalog for more wonderful educational software.

Motes Educational Software, PO Box 575, Siloam Springs AR 72761, (501) 524-8741. Email: 73757.1111 @compuserve.com. Internet site: http:ourworld. compuserve.com/homepages/ schoolmom. They offer *School-Mom* children's educational software. It's a very wholesome and comprehensive program that teaches most subjects to most grade levels. Available in Windows and on CD-ROM.

Nordic Software, PO Box 6007, Lincoln NE 68506-0007. (402) 488-5086. FAX (402) 488-2914. Internet site: http://www.nordicsoftware. com/Email: info@ nordicsoftware.com

This company has educational software for math, En-

glish, vocabulary, foreign language, and preschool learning.

One of their bestselling titles is *Turbo Math Facts*™ ($49.95) which is an interactive car race that builds math skills for ages 5 to 12. *Turbo Math* recognizes when a student is having difficulty and struggling with a problem. If the user misses the same problem, he will have to report to the Pit Stop for a tune-up.

Tackle English™ ($59.95) for ages 8 to 15 is an interactive football game that teaches capitalization, punctuation, and other grammar skills.

The Preschool Parade™ (49.95) puts the user in a colorful, musical parade that teaches counting, the alphabet, shapes and colors, and more.

All of the software mentioned is available for Macintosh or IBM and on CD-ROM.

Christian homeschoolers will be happy about their new division, Family Interactive, that is producing Christian educational software materials. Now available is *Noah's Ark*™ ($59.95). Kids ages 3 to 7 can learn about what life was like on the ark. The Bible story, along with song lyrics, jigsaw puzzles, and conversation, help children become aware of Noah's purpose. Available on CD-ROM for Macintosh or Windows. **See ad page 75.**

NovaNet Campus™, University Communications, Inc., 3895 N. Business Center Drive, Suite 120, Tucson AZ 85705. Toll-free 1-800-243-7758. FAX (520) 888-8729. Internet site: http://www.nn.com/campus. Email: campus@nn.com.

This company offers a new educational software service that is available to home-schoolers and others. Campus offers over 1,200 lessons ranging from third grade through high school in many subject areas. Lessons are offered with pre-tests and post-tests, and scores are stored for each student. It's reasonably priced at three price levels, and you can try it out for a month with no long-term commitment necessary.

The service was reviewed in *Inside Tucson Business,* April 1, 1996, which interviewed Mrs. Loutzenheiser, a homeschooling mother who was using the service. She said, "For me, I don't have to search to try to find the material." The software was able to determine her son's skills and place him at the appropriate level. For more information, call the toll-free number or access their Web site.

Packard Bell Interactive Software, 1201 3rd Ave., #2301, Seattle WA 98101. (206) 654-4100. Packard Bell has developed a line of interactive educational software. The software is often available through your local software store. The titles described are available on CD-ROM that runs on either Windows or Macintosh.

For ages 3 to 7, there's *The Learning Library,* that actually is three softwares in one: *Emily Culpepper, The Pirate Who Wouldn't Wash,* and *The Wrong-Way Around the World.* These units teach reading, comprehension, spelling, and thinking skills.

For ages 4 to 9, there's *The Little Engine, Milly Fitzwilly's Mouse Catcher, Little Red Riding Hood, Dinosaur in the Garden,* and *Goldilocks and the Three Bears.* Each of these teaches reading, comprehension, spelling, and critical thinking skills through entertaining, interactive stories.

Parsons Technology, One Parsons Dr., PO Box 100, Hiawatha IA 52233-0100.

(319) 395-9626. Toll-free 1-800-223-6925. FAX (319) 395-7449. Interesting product: *QuickVerse®* for Windows. The newest way to study the Bible. You can locate any word or phrase in the Bible in seconds with QuickSearch feature. You can also study numerous Bible translations simultaneously (translations additional fee). You can create a personalized study Bible, $49.

Penton Overseas, Inc., 2470 Impala Drive, Carlsbad CA 92008-7226. (619) 431-0060. Toll-free 1-800-748-5804. FAX (619) 431-8110. This company specializes in foreign language learning tools. Materials are available for ages 5+, and there are books, audios, videos, CD-ROMs, games and more.

An award-winning program is *Lyric Language®*, which has won a SIVA award, a Benjamin Franklin Award, and more. This series is loved by children, and available on video, audio, and CD-ROM. Languages available: French, German, Italian, Japanese (audio & video only), and Spanish. Audios, $9.95 each, videos $14.95 each, and CD-ROMs $49.95 each.

School Zone Publishing, 1819 Industrial Drive, PO Box 777, Grand Haven MI 49417. (616) 846-5030. FAX (616) 846-6181. Toll-free 1-800-253-0564. Educational CD-ROM for children age 3+ to teach alphabet skills and phonics. Superb color, excellent animation, playful sounds, and fun rewards give high entertainment value to an educational mission. Activities include letter sequence, animated alphabet song, hidden letter scenes, 78 coloring pages, fire house game, 15 mazes, 10 dot-to-dots with 60 ways to connect, and two original movies ($#9.95). Free catalog.
See ad page 48.

Show Me Math, PO Box 7452, Overland Park KS 66207. (913) 383-5005. *Show Me Math™* software shows children how to build over 85 vital math skills. It's a system that allows each child to work at a difficulty level that will challenge his or her problem-solving ability. It's not just a program with math problems. It's an interactive software that shows children step-by-step how to solve almost any mathematical category. $59.

Socially Redeeming Software, 1717 E. Union Hills #1034, Phoenix AZ 85024.

(602) 482-3161. *Cursive 3D Pro* is a program that helps children, with or without learning disabilities, to learn cursive handwriting. This program sets the cursive alphabet on water and demonstrates the spacing of each letter through visual images of sky, above and below the water. Cursive 3D Pro is aesthetically pleasing, soothing to the eyes, and the directions are simple.

Sound Software, 3905 Coronado, Plano TX 75074. (214) 516-1328. This company offers an educational series that starts with phonics for K-1; math, reading, spelling and vocabulary for grades 1-5; and continues with activities through fifth grade. In all, it's 20 programs for under $100: PC CD-ROM version $69; PC Sound Blaster version $99; Macintosh 1.44 version $99.

Sycamore Tree, 2179 Meyer Place, Costa Mesa CA 92627. (714) 650-4466 for information about products and services. For ordering, call or FAX toll-free 1-800-779-6750. Internet site: http://www. sycamoretree.com/home.html

In addition to full curriculums, The Sycamore Tree offers individual materials in their comprehensive 112-page catalog. There's a wide selection of over 3,000 items. There are materials for Bible study, character development, math, grammar, science, social science, arts and crafts, music, cooking and nutrition, games and puzzles, toys, videos and even parent helps. The catalog is free if you mention this book.

Educational software shareware is available in many subjects. **See ad page 50.**

Timberdoodle Company, E1510 Spencer Lake Road, Shelton WA 98584. (360) 426-0672. Toll-free ordering 1-800-478-0672. FAX (360) 427-5625. Email: mailbag@ timberdoodle.com Internet site: http:/www.timberdoodle. com This company has a catalog specifically designed for homeschoolers. There are a lot of great and interesting materials here—check it out!

They have a lot of software and CD-ROMs. *The Way Things Work,* which was awarded Best Software for Children, Oppenheim Toy Profile, combines the information of a book with animation and video clips showing the operations of machines and how they work, CD-ROM for Macintosh or IBM, $42.

They have foreign language on CD-ROMs—Hebrew or Japanese ($65); Spanish, French or German ($75). Also available is piano instruction on CD-ROM, the *Piano Discover System Deluxe*, $250.

A good spelling system on CD-ROM is *Spell It 3*, that uses 5 games and 3,600 words in 6 levels of difficulty, $40.

They have a *World Discovery Deluxe* CD-ROM for teaching geography that they believe is a gem! This CD has 75 current colorful maps, a dozen different games, four levels of quizzes, dozens of countries jigsaw puzzle options, greetings in native tongue for many countries, and more. This CD-ROM works on Macintosh or IBM, $40.

Transparent Language®, 22 Proctor Hill Road, PO Box 575, Hollis NJ 03049. (603) 465-2230. Toll-free orders 1-800-752-1767. FAX (603) 465-2779.Email:admin @transparent.com

This company specializes in software that teaches foreign languages. They have a series called *Language Now!* that helps you learn the new language without the boring drills, but instead with entertaining stories from a native speaker of that language. Each language comes on a CD-ROM for $129 or a diskette with an audio cassette for $99: Spanish, Russian, French, German, Italian, Latin, and ESL.

There are also numerous other foreign language educational materials in their catalog.

WFF 'N PROOF Learning Games Associates, 1490-FJ South Blvd., Ann Arbor MI 48104-4699. (313) 665-2269. Equations game for the computer—IBM or Apple. Satisfaction guaranteed. Ask for catalog.

Write Away!

English Composition and Word Processing

The step-by-step format in this 300-page textook facilitates self-paced and independent study. Lessons include an introduction to *Windows*™ as well as word processing, sentence and paragraph construction, journal writing, research papers, resumes, job applications, and business letters.
Required: *Windows*™ 3.1 or '95 and *Student Writing Center*™

For information contact:
**Abbott Computer Training Inc.
P.O. Box 77527
Steamboat Springs
CO 80477
Ph: (970) 870-6673
E-Mail:
abbott@cmn.net**

Noah's Ark

*N*oah's Ark teaches children counting, simple spelling, matching and helps develop early thinking skills with ten different activities. Children can wander freely though Noah's Ark to discover learning activities that relate to the story of Noah. Additional skill levels build on learned activities so children can continue to learn while parents are away from the computer. Noah's Ark is a CD-ROM for Mac and Windows; Ages 3-7.

Family Interactive

Special Introductory Offer!!!
• Please call or fax for pricing •

System Requirements: MAC - Color Mac, 4MB of RAM, 6.0.8 or greater; **WINDOWS** - 386 or better, 4MB of RAM, Windows 3.1 or later, mouse, SVGA, sound card.

Family Interactive • P.O. Box 6638 • Lincoln, NE 68506 • Phone: 800-275-6159 • Fax: 402-488-2914

Chapter Six
MAGAZINES & GOOD READING BOOKS

Magazines are excellent supplemental educational materials. Some children's magazines are designed for certain fields, such as history, science, and astronomy. There are magazines written entirely by children, which is an inspirational way for kids to see their writing potential by looking at what other children write.

This chapter also lists sources for good reading books for children. And as all homeschoolers know—don't forget the library!

Atrium Society Publications, PO Box 816, Middlebury, VT 05753. Toll Free 1-800-848-6021. These globally-aware books concerning peace have received the Benjamin Franklin Award for Peace Education.

Bluestocking Press, PO Box 2030, Shingle Springs CA 95682-2030. (916) 621-1123. Toll-free 1-800-959-8586. FAX (916) 642-9222. Publishes two books that are very useful: *How to Stock a Home Library Inexpensively,* 3rd edition, by Jane A. Williams. This widely used book is now in its third edition. This is a one-of-a-kind guide on the subject of inexpensive book collecting that includes resources for discount book buying—both mail order and stores. "Perfect for all book lover who long for a complete home library and lack the funds to stock one."— *Library Journal.* Another useful book is *Books Children*

Love by Elizabeth L. Wilson. This book is designed to put quality children's literature into the hands of parents. It lists hundreds of book from more than two dozen subject areas, with comments about each one. 320 pages, $14.95. **See ad page 27.**

Bob Jones University Press, Greenville SC 29614. Toll-free 1-800-845-5731. Appropriate graded reading material for young people (K-12), listed with brief descriptions and sources in their catalog. All materials selected according to a Christian viewpoint. Examples of supplemental reading books in their catalog: *Champion of Freedom: Charles Ludwig*, the biography of the author of *Uncle Tom's Cabin*, for teens, $7.99; *Florence Nightingale: The Lady of the Lamp,* teens, $4.99; *The Cranky Blue Crab*, illustrated storybook for ages 2-6, $5.49. Call toll-free number to order or inquire.

Boodle: By Kids for Kids, PO Box 1049, Portland IN 47371. *Boodles* is a school-year quarterly magazine with stories, poems, articles, puzzles and more for children ages 6-12. This magazine has been chosen to be included in the *Best of the Best for Children,* a guide by the American Library Association. Subscription is $10 for 1 year, 4 issues.

Boy Scouts of America, Magazine Division, 1325 Walnut Hill Lane, Irving TX 75083-3096. (214) 580-2000. Publishers of *Boy's Life*, subscription $7.80 to Boy Scouts, $15.60 per year (12 issues) to others.

Bradshaw Publishers, PO Box 277, Bryn Mawr CA 92318. (909) 796-6766. *Bible Stories for Early Readers* are published by this company. For only $4.99, the small paperback books are colorfully illustrated, use progressive word building techniques, and teach wholesome Bible stories like *The Good Samaritan,* and *Naaman Finds a Cure.* Contact the above address for more information.

Caxton Printers, Ltd., 312 Main St., Caldwell ID 83605-3299. (208) 459-7421. FAX (208) 459-7450. Toll-free 1-800-657-6465. They have best-loved titles such as *Paul Bunyan Swings His Axe* and *Tall Timber Tales,* each $11.95.

Children's Art Foundation, PO Box 83, Santa Cruz CA

95063. Toll-free 1-800-447-4569. *Stone Soup Magazine: the magazine by young writers and artists* is a literary and fine art publication of work by preteens. It has a reputation as one of the finest publishers of children's works. Editor Gerry Mandell told *U.S. Air Magazine*, "Our goal is to publish writing that really speaks to kids, that makes them want to read and want to write." Subscription, 1 year, 5 issues, $26.

Children's Better Health Institute, 1100 Waterway Blvd., PO Box 567, Indianapolis IN 46206. (317) 636-8881. This publisher produces fine magazines for children ages 2 to preteen.

Turtle, ages 2-5, is full of hidden pictures, mazes, colorful stories, poems and pictures by their readers. *Humpty Dumpty*, for ages 4-6, has stories, crafts, puzzles, games, and more. Children's *Playmate*, for ages 6-8, has colorfully illustrated stories for beginning readers, as well as puzzles, games and activities. *Jack and Jill*, for ages 7-10, has been published for over 50 years. It has great fiction, reader participation pages, games, and activities. *Child Life*, for ages 9-11, has multicultural stories, puzzles, games, and a chance for the readers to get published. *Children's Digest,* for preteens, features contemporary fiction, features about nutrition, sports, and the environment.

U*S*KIDS, A Weekly Reader Magazine, for ages 5-10, has lots of great illustrations and photography. There's stores, world news, and activities.

Children's Books at Discount Prices, PO Box 19069, Denver CO 80219. (303) 237-4989. I first saw this company at the Arizona Home School Curriculum Fair this year. They were swamped with people in their booth all the time. The reason: they have great books for kids at discount prices. Shop their catalog and save!

Children's Small Press Collection, 719 N. Fourth Ave., Ann Arbor MI 48104. (313) 668-8056. Toll-free 1-800-221-8056. Their catalog has hard to find, well-chosen books and music for tots to teens, and also resources for parents, teachers, and family support professionals. The catalog has books in the areas of: creativity, self-sufficiency, science & the environment, self-esteem; fiction, multicultural, history, family structure, parenting, counseling, values, music and foreign language.

Good reading books from this catalog are: *Through Her Eyes: A True Story of Love, Miracles and Realities* by Linda Rivers, about a girl who lived fully her 14 years, with inspiration about positive thinking and fulfilling those dreams, $7.95; *The Maybe Garden,* "This is a universal story of the power of creativity to infuse serious knowledge with life."—*Publisher's Weekly*, $7.95.

Children's Television Workshop, 1 Lincoln Plaza, New York NY 10023. (212) 595-3456. This company produces wonderful magazines for children. *Sesame Street,* for ages 2-6, features games, puzzles, and children's stories; (10 issues for $19.90). *Kid City,* ages 6-10, contains collections of articles and projects for children who are beginning to read; (10 issues, $16.97); *3-2-1 Contact,* for ages 8-14, award-winning stories about nature, animals, the environment and technology; (10 issues, $17.97).

Cobblestone Publishing, Inc., 7 School Road, Peterborough NH 03458-1454. (603) 924-7209. Toll-free 1-800-821-0115. FAX (603) 924-7280.

Internet site: http://www.cobblestonepub.com.

This company publishes a group of beautiful and informative magazines for young people. *Cobblestone* is the history magazine for young people. Each issue is packed with interesting, lively, and historically accurate articles. (1 year, 9 issues, $24.95.) *Odyssey* is the science magazine that shows readers that science is sensational. The magazine has interviews with scientists, book reviews, activities, and contests. (1 year, 9 issues, $24.95.) *FACES* is a magazine that shows readers world cultures. Some issues focus on a country or group of people, others may offer diversity on a particular issue (such as pottery throughout the world). (1 year, 9 issues, $23.95). *Calliope* is a world history magazine for young people. Each issue has a theme, and then articles to develop that theme. (1 year, 5 issues, $18.95.)

Concord Review: A Quarterly Review of Essays by Students of History, PO Box 661, Concord MA 01742. (508) 331-5007. Email: fitzhugh@tcr.org

The Concord Review is the <u>only</u> journal in the world to publish the academic work of secondary students. Since 1987, they have published 286 history essays from student authors in the United States and 19 other countries. Many of the students have sent reprints of their essays with the college applications. They welcome materials from homeschooled students. **See ad page 81.**

Consumers Union of U.S., Inc., PO Box 57777, Yonkers NY 10703. (914) 378-2000. This organization publishes the magazine *Zillions*, formerly called *Penny Power*. This magazine is for consumer education of children. Too many times children are not taught how to handle themselves in the marketplace. This magazine helps teach them how to conduct a simple business transaction like an adult, and how to be aware of what their money is spent on. Subscription, $16 for 1 year, 6 issues, ages 7-12.

Cricket Magazine Group, PO Box 7434, Red Oak IA 51591-4434. Order toll-free 1-800-827-0227. They are publishers of a group of excellent magazines for children ages infants to 14 years.

Babybug, for infants from 6 months to toddlers of 2 years, is a board-book magazine with colorful illustrations and simple rhymes that parents can read to their babies. *Ladybug*, for ages 2-6, is a colorful magazine filled with games, songs, poems, and a removable 4-page activity insert. *Spider*, for ages 6-9, is for independent young readers. It is filled with beautiful illustrations, games, activities, puzzles, stories, and projects. *Cricket*, for ages 9-14, includes drawing, poetry, story and photography contests, as well as writing by some of the world's best writers. Each magazine is $2.75 per issue; all magazines except *Babybug* have 12 issues per year; *Babybug* has 9 issues per year.

Enslow Publishers, Inc., 44 Fadem Road, Box 699, Springfield NJ 07081-0699. (201) 379-8890. FAX (201) 379-7940. Toll-free ordering 1-800-398-2504. Internet site: http://www.enslow.com

I believe that young people will be better readers if they are given materials to read that interest them. For boys, that might mean reading about sports heroes. This company has a *Sports Greats* series of books that should interest these readers, ages 9-15. There are biographies about Karl Malone, Shaquille O'Neal,

The Concord Review—Varsity Academics

I very much like and support what you are doing with *The Concord Review*. It's original, important, and *greatly needed*, now more than ever, with the problem of historic illiteracy growing steadily worse among the high school generation nearly everywhere in the country.

David McCullough, Historian

The Concord Review is simply the best thing to happen to support the case for excellence in writing in high school history classes in the past fifteen years.

Bernadette Glaze, Head of History, Mount Vernon High School

It has frequently occurred to me that people interested in developing history standards should also read through the first six volumes of *The Concord Review*.

Albert Shanker, President, American Federation of Teachers

WE HAVE PUBLISHED 286 SERIOUS HISTORY ESSAYS (AVERAGE 5,000 WORDS) BY HIGH SCHOOL STUDENTS FROM TWENTY COUNTRIES IN THE LAST EIGHT YEARS. CALL, WRITE OR EMAIL US FOR OUR "FORM TO ACCOMPANY ESSAYS" OUR "SUBSCRIPTION FORM" AND A FREE ISSUE.

The articles in *The Concord Review* are substantial and appropriately challenging, yet "intellectually digestible" for all students, not just the gifted few in an AP section...In addition, they are always impressed that students like themselves can and do produce such high-quality work.

Broeck N. Oder, Head of History, Santa Catalina School

I was pleased to learn that the author of one of the essays, Sarah Valkenburgh, is coming to Dartmouth in the fall. I read her essay with great interest and was deeply impressed by its quality.

James O. Freedman, President, Dartmouth College

The Concord Review • Post Office Box 661, Concord, MA 01742
(800) 331-5007 Internet: fitzhugh@tcr.org Website: http://www.tcr.org

Charles Barkley, David Robinson, Magic Johnson, Michael Jordan, Patrick Ewing, and more, each $14.35. Also there's a series, *Countdown to Space*, for ages 9-15, that has books about Apollo 11, Apollo 13, Challenger, Columbia, and more, each $14.35.

Free Spirit Publishing, Inc., 400 1st Avenue North Ste. 616, Minneapolis MN 55401. (612) 338-2068. FAX (612) 337-5050. *The Kid's Guide to Social Action: How to Solve the Social Problems You Choose—and Turn Creative Thinking into Positive Actions*, for ages 10+, $14.95. This book was called an "outstanding children's book" by *Parenting Magazine.*

Great Christian Books, 229 South Bridge Street, PO Box 8000, Elkton MD 21922-8000. (410) 392-0930. Toll-free orders 1-800-775-5422. FAX (410) 392-3103. Email: gcb@ssnet.com Internet site: http:www.GreatChristianBooks.com Send for special catalog *Homeschool Warehouse.* Satisfaction guaranteed. This is a great one-stop shopping place for homeschooling books of all kinds!

Great source for good reading books for kids. They have numerous classics: *Anne of Green Gables* ($2.75); *Winnie-the-Pooh* ($8.75); and popular titles such as the Christy fiction series, the *Chronicles of Narnia*, and more.

Highlights for Children (and Essential Learning Products Company), PO Box 269, 2300 W. 5th Ave., Columbus OH 43272-0002. (614) 486-0695. FAX (614) 487-2700. Toll-free 1-800-255-9517. *Highlights for Children* is a five-star children's magazine that has been thrilling readers for two generations with stories, cartoons, biographies, music, history, science, crafts and activities, and submissions from readers. I loved this magazine as a child, and my daughter loved it also! Subscription: 1 year, 12 issues, $29.64. Sample issue free.

Holt Associates, 2269 Massachusetts Ave, Cambridge MA 02140. (617) 864-3100. FAX (617) 864-9235. John Holt is considered the father of modern homeschooling. If you're reading this book, you've no doubt heard much about him. He authored ten books about education including the classic, *How Children Fail.* In 1977 he founded *Growing Without*

Schooling, a magazine dedicated to supporting home educators. He also founded *John Holt's Bookstore,* a catalog through which he sold books about education that he thought were especially good.

John Holt's catalog used to contain a lot of reading material for children, which has now been discontinued. However, there is a list available of these recommended titles, called *John Holt's Reading List,* $2.

Lifetime Books & Gifts, 3900 Chalet Suzanne Dr., Lake Wales FL 33853. (941) 676-6311. Toll Free for ordering 1-800-377-0390. From their *The Always Incomplete Resource Guide & Catalog,* ($3) they offer a host of quality educational materials. This Christian based catalog has many highly recommended books and other educational materials.

Merlyn's Pen, PO Box 1058, Greenwich RI 02818. Toll-free 1-800-247-2027. This magazine, which publishes the works by students in grades 6-12, has won a Parents' Choice Award for four consecutive years. Editor James Stahl said, "*Merlyn's Pen* inspires young adults to find and honor their own articulate voices." Two editions available: the middle school edition for grades 6-9, and the senior edition for grades 9-12. Subscription: 1 year, 4 issues, $21. Call toll-free number for official cover sheet for submissions.

National Wildlife Federation, 1400 16th St., NW, Washington DC 20036-2266. FAX (703) 442-7332. Order toll-free 1-800-432-6564. Customer service toll-free 1-800-822-9919. TDD toll-free 1-800-435-3543.

Publishers of *Ranger Rick* (ages 6-12, $15, 12 issues) and *Your Big Backyard* (ages 3-5, $14, 12 issues) magazines that give children a colorful, magical journey into the world of nature.

Parents' Choice, Box 185, Waban, MA 02168. (617) 965-5913. This non-profit organization publishes a highly recommended quarterly newsletter that reviews media for children: toys, books, software, records, and movies. Their advisory board members are from many academically acclaimed institutions: Brown University, Yale, Harvard School of Medicine, and many more. A subscription is $20.00.

Chapter Six: Magazines & Reading Books

Prufrock Press™, PO Box 8813, Waco TX 76714-8813. (817) 756-3337. FAX (817) 756-3339. Toll-free ordering 1-800-998-2208. Toll-free FAX for ordering 1-800-240-0333. Internet site: http://www.purfrock.com

This company has a catalog of creative teaching ideas, including items to help teach gifted students. They have a *Creative Kids Magazine,* in which everything in it is by kids! To download authors' guidelines, go to their home pages on the Internet.

Weekly Reader Corporation, 245 Long Hill Road, PO Box 2791, Middletown CT 06457-9291. (860) 638-2400. Customer service toll-free 1-800-446-3355. *The Weekly Reader* has been a favorite for kids for more than a generation! This news magazine for grades K-6 has current events, stories, and study skills. These magazines are available only in group lots, so it's something that home-schoolers could do with their support group.

Chapter Seven

BIBLE EDUCATION & CHRISTIAN MATERIALS

This chapter lists companies that produce Bible study materials, Bible-based curriculums, Bible-based correspondence schools, Bible toys and games, Christian reading materials, Christian character development materials, and other products produced specifically for the Christian home.

Alpha Omega Publications, 300 N. McKemy Ave, Chandler AZ 85226-2618. (602) 438-2717 Toll-free 1-800-622-3070 FAX (602) 940-8924. Email:aop@home-schooling.com Internet site: http: www.home-schooling.com. This company has an extensive range of products available for homeschoolers. In fact, they produce an 88-page full-color catalog! All materials are written with Christian education in mind.

New in this catalog is Christian education software. For preschoolers there's *Rev-Up*™ *for Reading, Rev-Up*™ *for Writing*, and *Rev-Up*™ *for Arithmetic*. The programs contain charming, animated characters from the *Amazing Bible* video series, and use traditional teaching methods coupled with advanced CD-ROM technology. Available on CD-ROM for windows, $14.95 each.

Bible Builder and *Captain Bible* teach Bible skills with colorful, animated scenes and different skill levels. This was the winner of the 1993 "Reader's Choice Award" by *Christian Computing Magazine*. CD-ROM for IBM, $14.95 each.

Bible studies are offered in LIFEPAC curriculum format for grades 1 to 9. Home-schoolers who are familiar with LIFEPACS will be pleased with their new LIFEPAC Gold format, which is full color.

Additional Bible resources offered are the *Parables for Kids Series* with Adam Raccoon. Cartoon characters will teach Biblical lessons in these beautifully illustrated books for ages 4 to 7. Each $8.99.

Inspirational videos include the *In the Beginning*, a 3-video set for $34.95; and *Jesus from the Gospel*, 3-video set for $34.95.

Alta Vista Curriculum, 12324 Rd 37, Madera CA 93638. (209) 645-4083. Toll-free 1-800-544-1397. Alta Vista's goal is to provide a Biblically based curriculum founded on a Christian world view, directed toward children of all learning styles, and committed to the idea that learning is best achieved through integrating the academic subjects. There are four levels: Level A is Preschool through 1st grade; Level B is 1st-3rd grades; Level C is 4th-6th grades; Level D is 7th-9th grades. Units are $95 each and include student text and worksheets.

Bible Study Guide for All Ages, PO Box 2608, Russellville AR 72811. The *Bible Study Guide for All Ages* is for classes, study groups, and family devotionals. It comes with instructions, lessons, study helps, drills & maps, visuals, and an audio cassette tape.

Bob Jones University Press, Greenville SC 29614-0001. Toll-free 1-800-845-5731. FAX toll-free 1-800-524-8398. Free home school brochure, call 1-800-739-8199. This company offers complete curriculum for grades K-12, with abundant helps for the teachers. It is a thoroughly Christian program with high-quality materials. Supplemental Christian materials also available. Free catalog—just call toll-free number.

Bible studies available for all levels. For grades 2-6, there's the series *Bible Truths*, which give Bible lessons and explores doctrinal truths, $6.50 each. For this series, there are also Bible tests, $1.95 per level, and *Bible Music Cassettes,* $7.50 per level.

Bradshaw Publishers, PO Box 277, Bryn Mawr CA 92318. (909) 796-6766. *Bible Stories for Early Readers* are published by this company. For only $4.99 each plus shipping and handling, the small paperback books are colorfully illustrated, use progressive word building techniques, and teach wholesome Bible stories like *The Good Samaritan*, and *Naaman Finds a Cure*. Contact the above address for more information.

Bread Ministries Inc., PO Box 1017, Arcadia FL 33821-1017. Publishes *Bread for God's Children*, a Christian publication that teaches Christian values (available in English and Spanish).

Builder Books, PO Box 99, Riverside WA 98849. (509) 826-6021. Toll-free orders 1-800-260-5461. Their catalog has a section titled, "Bible Character Building," featuring titles like, *Proverbs for Parenting*, *Your Story Hour* cassettes, Christian character materials, and more.

Children's Bible Hour, Box 1, Grand Rapids MI 49501. Internet site: http://www.gospelcom.net/cbh/ They offer a wide variety of Christian valued materials.

Christian Liberty Academy Satellite Schools, 502 W. Euclid Ave, Arlington Heights IL 60004. (847) 259-4444. FAX (847) 259-2941. The Christian Liberty Academy Satellite Schools has over 22,000 students in 50 states and 56 foreign counties. Grades 1-12. They offer flexible plans according to the parents' needs. One plan keeps the administrative records with them. With the other plan, the parents keep the records. Either way, you can select textbooks from 25 different publishers, have basic skill testing, custom designed curriculum, plus materials and guidance.

Christian Life Workshops (CLW), Box 2250, Gresham OR 97030. (503) 667-3942. This organization has a plethora of books, manuals, audio/visual materials, workshops, organizers and other materials for order.

Color the Classics, PO Box 440, Silver Springs NY 14550. *Color the Classics* is a biographical coloring book and cassette tape to help kids learn to love the music and lives of Christ-centered composers. Ages 4-11. $12.95, volumes 1, 2, 3 & 4.

Creation's Child, PO Box 3004 #44, Corvallis OR

97339. (541) 758-3413. They offer Christian oriented time lines that show the lifespan of people of the *Bible* and other world historical events.

Creative Home Teaching, PO Box 152581, San Diego CA 92105. (619) 263-8633. Their catalog contains Bible and character-building materials.

Crossings®, 6550 E. 30th St., PO Box 6325, Indianapolis IN 46206-6325. (317) 541-8920. Crossings® is the book club for today's Christian families.

Davidsons Music, 6726 Metcalf, Shawnee Mission KS 66204. (913) 262-6533. Piano course for Christians. Gives complete foundation in music and emphasizes Christian values and concepts. Preparatory book $7.95. Two cassettes give further explanations, demonstrate music and give advice and encouragement, $10.95 each or $21.90 for both. Book plus both cassettes $27.

Doorposts, Suite 372, PO Box 1610, Clackamas OR 97015. (503) 698-7973. Doorposts is a family business. They began several years ago with a hand-drawn *If-Then Chart* on their kitchen wall. Some friends saw it, made a copy of it, and then passed copies on to other families in the church. The home business has continued to grow and expand and add products. Send for their newest catalog.

The *If-Then Chart* is a 16" x 22" chart designed to help parents be more consistent in disciplining their children. It helps parents to know what to do when they disobey. The chart is divided into three columns. the left-hand column lists kinds of misbehavior (arguing, complaining, teasing, hitting, etc.) illustrated with a simple cartoon. The center column gives a Scripture verse related to each misbehavior. The third column is blank so that parents can write in the agreed-upon consequences for each misbehavior. This helps parents be very consistent and it is so clear that even two-year-olds can understand: $4.50.

The *Blessings Chart* is a 16" x 22" chart designed to help parents acknowledge and reward godly attitudes and behavior. This is a chart that balances to the *If-Then Chart*. $5.

A new product from Doorposts is the book *Plants Grown Up*. This enormous book (8 1/2" x 11", 536 pages, $40) contains hundreds of practical activities and Bible study ideas for sons to prepare for their future roles as employees, husbands, fathers, and church leaders. The book provides lessons in such moral issues as self-control of the body and appetite, fleeing temptation, patience, developing Godly relationships, and giving to those in need. For Christian homeschoolers with sons, this is an important book.

Another new book by Doorposts is *For Instruction in Righteousness*, (8 1/2" x 11", $25) which is a handbook to help parents use the Bible as they train their children. Moral issues discussed are pride, self-righteousness, hypocrisy, judging others, jealousy, depression, impatience, anger, gluttony, drunkenness, gossip, bitterness, insensitivity, and more.

Families Honoring Christ, Earl & Diane Rodd, 2180 Northland Ave, Lakewood OH 44107. *Training for Royalty*, book describing the Biblical Basis for home education, $5; Families, *Dating and the Bible,* pamphlet, $1; *Disciplineship of Young Children,* pamphlet, $1; *Training Kings,* pamphlet, $1.

Gateway Films/ Vision Video, 2030 Wentz Church Road, PO Box 540, Worcester PA 19490-0540. (610) 584-1893. FAX (610) 584-4610. Toll-free ordering 1-800-523-

0226. Their catalog contains wonderful videos for children, including the *Children's Heroes of the Bible* series, with titles about Jesus, Joseph, Moses, David, Elijah, Jeremiah, and Esther, $7.95 each.

God's World Publications Inc., 85 Tunnel Rd. Innsbruck Mall, PO Box 2330, Asheville NC 28802-2330. Toll-free 1-800-951-5437. Publish a weekly current events newspaper for children from a Christian perspective. Prices vary. Please call toll free with your inquiries.

Good News Publishers, Crossway Books, 1300 Crescent St., Wheaton IL 60187. FAX (708) 682-4785. Toll-free ordering 1-800-323-3890. This is one of America's favorite Christian publishers. Two of their newer titles that may interest homeschoolers: *The Song of the King,* by popular writer Max Lucado, author of *Tell Me the Story* and *Tell Me the Secrets,* this new book is for children and teaches them that if they follow the song of God, it will lead them through darkness to truth, $12.99; and *Ten Secrets for a Successful Family,* shows parents how to consistently and creatively teach Christian family values in the home, $17.99.

Great Christian Books, 229 South Bridge Street, PO Box 8000, Elkton MD 21922-8000. (410) 392-0930. Toll-free orders 1-800-775-5422. FAX (410) 392-3103. Email: gcb@ssnet.com Internet site: http:www.GreatChristianBooks.com Send for special catalog *Homeschool Warehouse.* Satisfaction guaranteed. This is a great one-stop shopping place for homeschooling books of all kinds!

Numerous Christian materials available in this catalog. There are Bible storybooks, books by the popular author Max Lucado, Bible curriculums, and much more.

Green Pastures Press, 7102 Lynn Road NE, Minerva OH 44657. (33) 895-3291. Publishers and distributors of books on old-fashioned values and virtues. Some of their new titles include: *Working with Wisdom,* which is a workbook with puzzles and short stories to reinforce character-building lessons (grade 3-4, $4); *101 Favorite Stories from the Bible* ($9.99); and *Timely Talks with Teenagers* ($2.50).

Growth Unlimited Inc. 36 Fairview, Battle Creek MI 49017 (616) 965-2229, Toll Free 1-800 441-7676, FAX 616-965-4522. This company publishes Christian based self-esteem books for children. *The Three Robots* series teach children about healthy self-esteem through three robot characters Pos, Semi-Pos, and Neg. Other books include ; *Friends to All, Joyful Lover,* and *Margaret of Castello.*

Hewitt Homeschooling Resources, PO Box 9, Washougal WA 98671-0009. (360) 835-8708. FAX (360) 835-8697. This company offers testing services, enrollment, and unit packages. The basic family registration is $25, and then units are $89 for grades 1-2, $137 for grades 3-8, and $90 per quarter for high school. Each unit includes an individualized curriculum guide, two hours of phone counseling, and a transcript for high school. Special needs package is available. Supplemental materials available. All materials are Christian based.

Howshall Home Publications, 9508 203rd Ave E, Sumner WA 98390. *Lifestyle of Learning* is the Christian journal that they publish. A one year subscription is $10.00.

Konos Curriculum, PO Box 1534, Richardson TX 75083. (214) 669-8337. Konos Curriculum is a widely used Christian character curriculum. Volume I teaches: attentiveness, obedience, orderliness, honor, trust, stewardship and patience; Volume II teaches: inquisitiveness, responsibility, generosity, courage, wisdom; Volume III teaches: self-control, determination, cooperation, honesty, creativity and resourcefulness. A six-hour seminar on cassette is available to train parents how to use the curriculum. Seminars can be scheduled for groups as well.

Landmark Distributors, PO Box 849, Fillmore CA 93015. (805) 524-3263. This is a family-owned organization that advocates the Principle Approach to American Christian Education. Basically, the Principle Approach is the ability to learn the Biblical origin of the subjects being taught. This approach develops Christian character. Their catalog of materials reflects this philosophy.

Landmark's Freedom Baptist Curriculum, 2222 E. Hinson Ave., Hinson City FL

33844-4902. FAX (941) 422-0188. Toll-free 1-800-700-LFBC. Total curriculum Pre-K through 12th grade. Baptist orientation. Individualized home school plans. Annual curriculum $225 for first child, each additional student $200. Record-keeping services also available.

Leadership Resources, PO Box 413, New Lenox IL 60451. (815) 485-4900. FAX (815) 485-4995. Toll-free ordering 1-800-572-6657. Publishes beautiful Bible study guides for the junior or senior high reader. The books have written exercises which promote self studying.

Lifetime Books & Gifts, 3900 Chalet Suzanne Dr., Lake Wales FL 33853. (941) 676-6311. Toll Free for ordering 1-800-377-0390. From their *The Always Incomplete Resource Guide & Catalog,* ($3) they offer a host of quality educational materials. There is a full section in their catalog called "General Creation Science for Children."

Melton Book Company, PO Box 23216, Waco TX 76702-3216. Toll-free ordering 1-800-441-0511. This company has a full catalog of Christian books for children and adults, with items of interest to home-schoolers such as children's Bibles, books, and videos. They have *My Little Prayer Series* for kids ages 2-5, a 4-volume set for $14.95. This company also has imprinting services and will imprint your name, initials, or church name onto almost any Bible.

Nordic Software, PO Box 6007, Lincoln NE 68506-0007. (402) 488-5086. FAX (402) 488-2914. Internet site: http://www.nordicsoftware. com/ Email: info@ nordicsoftware.com
Christian homeschoolers will be happy about their new division, Family Interactive, that is producing Christian educational software materials. Now available is Noah's Ark™ ($59.95). Kids ages 3 to 7 can learn about what life was like on the ark. The Bible story, along with song lyrics, jigsaw puzzles, and conversation, help children become aware of Noah's purpose. Available on CD-ROM for Macintosh or Windows. **See ad page 75.**

Our Christian Heritage, 7923 West 62nd Way, Arvade CO 8004. (303) 421-0444. Has a variety of Christian influenced textbooks and workbooks in the subjects of history, geography, and government.

Parsons Technology, One Parsons Dr., PO Box 100, Hiawatha IA 52233-0100. (319) 395-9626. Toll-free 1-800-223-6925. FAX (319) 395-7449. Interesting product: QuickVerse® for Windows. The newest way to study the Bible. You can locate any word or phrase in the Bible in seconds with QuickSearch feature. You can also study numerous Bible translations simultaneously (translations additional fee). You can create a personalized study Bible. $49.

Presbyterian Publishing Corporation, 3904 Produce Road, Louisville KY 40218. Toll-free 1-800-227-2872. *Christian Parenting: Raising Children in the Real World* is a practical, realistic, biblically based help for Christian parents.

Shady Grove Church, 1829 W. Shady Grove Church, Grand Prairie TX 75050. (214) 790-0800. This church offers a variety of curriculum counseling, testing and newsletters. Fellowships are available.

Sycamore Tree, 2179 Meyer

Place, Costa Mesa CA 92627. (714) 650-4466 for information about products and services. For ordering, call or FAX toll-free 1-800-779-6750. Internet site: http://www. sycamoretree.com/home.html
In addition to full curriculums, The Sycamore Tree offers individual materials in their comprehensive 112-page catalog. There's a wide selection of over 3,000 items. There are materials for Bible study, character development, math, grammar, science, social science, arts and crafts, music, cooking and nutrition, games and puzzles, toys, videos and even parent helps. A helpful touch on this catalog is that Bible-based materials are indicated by a special symbol. The catalog is free if you mention this book.
See ad page 50.

Timberdoodle Company, E1510 Spencer Lake Road, Shelton WA 98584. (360) 426-0672. Toll-free ordering 1-800-478-0672. FAX (360) 427-5625. Email: mailbag@ timberdoodle.com Internet site: http:/www.timberdoodle. com This company has a catalog specifically designed for homeschoolers. There's a lot of great and interesting materials here—check it out!

They have a Christian Music series called *Hide 'Em in Your Heart*, Volumes I and II, which is Scripture set to music. Songs range from soothing, mellow, to lively. Each cassette is $7, each CD is $10.

They offer Bible software: *Bible Words for Windows* on CD-ROM. This is the ultimate database search tool for the Bible, $270.

Treasure! MSC 1000, 829 S. Shields, Fort Collins CO 80251-3541. Toll-free 1-800-284-0158. Offers a catalog that has many Bible and Christian oriented materials.

Triangle Press, 23 5th Ave SE, Conrad MT 59425. (406) 278-5664. Publishers of *Bible Truths for Little Children* (Volumes I-V, $5.98 ea.), which is a revision of a classic set written hundreds of years ago. The series is highly moralistic, lively and involving.

Trivium Pursuit, 139 Colorado St., Ste 168, Muscatine IA 52761. (309) 537-3641. *Teaching the Trivium:* A Quarterly Magazine of Classical Christian Education is available in back volumes and one current volume. The company has other educational materials available that are based on classical Christian educational philosophy.

Vic Lockman, Box 1916, Ramona CA 92065. This cartoonist has a series of books to teach how to draw cartoons, in a Christian perspective. *Cartooning for Young Children in a Christian Perspective,* Book I, $6.95; *The Big Book of Cartooning in Christian Perspective,* Book I, $12; Book II, Animals, $8, Big Book III,

Machines, $5.95.

Zondervan Directsource, Consumers Order Address: PO Box 668, Holmes PA 19043. This publishing company produces beautiful Bibles for juvenile to adult. *Tomie dePaola's Book of Bible Stories* is an especially richly illustrated children's book with large easy to read print for the text.

Chapter Eight
PARENTING & CHILD TRAINING BOOKS

Alliance for Parental Involvement in Education, Inc., PO Box 59, East Chatham NY 12060-0059. (518) 392-6900. Email: allpie@taconic.net Internet site: http://www.croton.com/allpie/ This is a parent-to-parent grassroots organization which assists people who wish to be involved in their children's education—whether that education takes place in public school, in private school, or at home.

Their book catalog has one child training book of interest: *Teaching Children Self-Discipline ... At Home and At School: New Ways Parents and Teachers Can Build Self-Control, Self-Esteem and Self-Reliance* gives solid and useful examples of how we can run our homes in a way that builds character and enhances self-esteem, hardcover, $17.95.

Children's Small Press Collection, 719 N. Fourth Ave., Ann Arbor MI 48104. (313) 668-8056. Toll-free 1-800-221-8056. Their catalog has hard to find, well-chosen books and music for tots to teens, and also resources for parents, teachers, and family support professionals. Good parenting books found in the catalog are: *Kids Can Cooperate: A Practical Guide to Teaching Problem Solving,* $12.95; *Without Spanking or Spoiling* (2nd edition) with lots of ideas for reducing conflicts without violence, appropriate for use with preschooler and toddlers as well as older children, $12.95; *Pick Up Your Socks ... & Other Skills Growing Children Need! A Practical Guide to Raising Responsible Children* with practical ideas for motivating kids and encouraging problem solving, $12.95.

Christian Life Workshops (CLW), Box 2250, Gresham OR 97030. (503) 667-3942. Through their publication *Our Family's Favorites* they have several training manuals for children like *Uncommon Courtesy for Kids, Rules for Young Friends, Hints on Child Training,* and *What the Bible Says About Child Training* (book and tape set). The materials are, of course Christian based.

Common Sense Press, PO Box 5863, Hollywood FL 33083. (305) 962-1930. FAX (305) 964-7644. They offer the two-cassette tape series *Improve Your Parenting* by Dr. Dale Simpson, a Christian psychologist. This program gives specific helps for achieving godly parenting. There are ideas in such areas as: communicating effectively with your child; producing wisdom in your child; the 3-question technique for all misbehavior; helping children learn self-control; getting kids to take responsibility; just saying "no" to power struggles, $18 for both tapes.

Creative Changes, Inc., 368 South 850 West, Orem UT 84058. (801) 226-5533. FAX (801) 226-3975. This company has a product called *Teaching Children Responsibility* that is 15 pages of work charts, job cards, system cards, incentives and rewards. Teaches good work habits for children of all ages. $5.95. Also offers the *Family Job Chart* that uses a wipe off marker and is easy to mount with magnets for your refrigerator. $5.95. There's also the *Creative Organizers System*™ that has reusable charts that are magnetized to use on the refrigerator. Includes several charts, tear away shopping list, phone message area, peel-off rainbow stickers. A great system, $19.95.

The Elijah Company, Route 2, Box 100-B, Crossville TN 38555. (615) 456-6284. FAX (615) 456-6384. Their catalog contains child training books.

Konos Curriculum, PO Box 1534, Richardson TX 75083. (214) 669-8337. Konos Curriculum is a widely used Christian character curriculum. Volume I teaches: attentiveness, obedience, orderliness, honor, trust, stewardship and patience; Volume II teaches: inquisitiveness, responsibility, generosity, courage wisdom; Volume III teaches: self-control, determination, cooperation, honesty, creativity and resourcefulness. A six-hour seminar on cassette is available to train parents how to use the curriculum. Live seminars can be scheduled for groups as well.

Lifetime Books & Gifts, 3900 Chalet Suzanne Dr., Lake Wales FL 33853. (941) 676-6311. Toll Free for ordering 1-800-377-0390. From their *The Always Incomplete Resource Guide & Catalog,* ($3) they offer a host of quality educational materials. Many training books and guides are available like, *Home Education: Training and Educating Children Under Nine,* and *How to Grow a Young Reader.*

Luvmour Family, PO Box 445, N. San Juan CA 95960. (916) 292-3858. Email: pathfinder@oro.net Internet site: http://www.oro.net/ ~pathfinder/pf/htm This family company has published two excellent books: *Towards Peace: Cooperative Games & Activities,* $8.95; and *Natural Learning Rhythms: How and When Children Learn,* $15.86.

The Moore Foundation, Box 1, Camas WA 98607. Raymond and Dorothy Moore have been called the "grandparents" of modern homeschooling. They are the authors of the classic homeschooling books: *Home Grown Kids, School Can Wait* and *Homeschool Burnout.* They are also the authors of *Home Built Discipline,* which helps parents develop initiative, self-control and responsibility in their children. They continue to conduct research and workshops internationally.

Parenting Press, PO Box 75267, 11065 5th Ave, NE, Suite F, Seattle WA 98125. (206) 364-2900. Toll-free 1-800-99-BOOKS. FAX (206) 364-0802. Internet site: http://www.parentbooks.com/ Parenting Press has an established reputation for fine books on parenting and child guidance. I especially like their philosophy of books that teach responsibility and cooperation to children and teach alternatives to spanking to parents. For instance, *Kids Can Cooperate: A Practical Guide to Teaching Problem Solving* (104 pages, $12.95); *Without Spanking or Spoiling: A Practical Approach to Toddler and Preschool Guidance* (2nd edition), that has sold more than 140,000 copies (128 pages, $14.95).

Redleaf Press, 450 N. Syndicate, Suite 5, St. Paul MN

55104-4125. (612) 641-0305. FAX toll-free 1-800-641-0115. Toll-free 1-800-423-8309. They have a 32-page full-color catalog of materials for parents and children, especially early childhood materials. I especially like their title, *The Kindness Curriculum: Introducing Children to Loving Values,* with over 60 imaginative activities for preschoolers and kindergarten, $13.95.

Sycamore Tree, 2179 Meyer Place, Costa Mesa CA 92627. (714) 650-4466 for information about products and services. For ordering, call or FAX toll-free 1-800-779-6750. Internet site: http://www. sycamoretree.com/home.html

In addition to full curriculums, The Sycamore Tree offers individual materials in their comprehensive 112-page catalog. There's a wide selection of over 3,000 items. The catalog is free if you mention this book. Child training books

include these titles: *How to Really Love Your Teenager; Raising Your Child, Not Your Voice; Parenting Teens with Love and Logic; Proverbs for Parenting; Making Children Mind Without Losing Yours* and more.

See ad page 50.

thisisit, inc., 905 S. Hohokam Drive, Tempe AZ 85281-5115. Toll-free 1-800-555-GROW (4769). This company has a program, *Succeeding with Difficult Children,* that helps parents deal with difficult children. Developed by a developmental pediatrician and a clinical psychologist, the program empowers parents to learn the skills necessary to deal with day to day situations, especially when dealing with children who have learning, behavioral, physical, attentional, emotional or social problems. This program is $129.95 and includes a set of 4 audio cassettes, a program guide, and an action manual.

Chapter Nine
HOW-TO-HOME-SCHOOL BOOKS

Alliance for Parental Involvement in Education, Inc., PO Box 59, East Chatham NY 12060-0059. (518) 392-6900. Email: allpie@taconic.net Internet site: http://www.croton.com/allpie/ This is a parent-to-parent grassroots organization which assists people who wish to be involved in their children's education—whether that education takes place in public school, in private school, or at home.

Their book catalog includes books for how-to-home school, such as *For New Homeschoolers* from Home Education Press, $2; *Should I Teach My Kids at Home? A Workbook for Parents,* $5; *College Admissions: A Guide for Homeschoolers,* $7.50. Other helpful how-to-homeschool titles available.

Alpha Omega Publications, 300 N. McKemy Ave, Chandler AZ 85226-2618. (602) 438-2717 Toll-free 1-800-622-3070 FAX (602) 940-8924. Email: aop@home-schooling. com Internet site: http:www. home-schooling.com. This company has an extensive range of products available for homeschoolers. In fact, they produce an 88-page full-color catalog! All materials are written with Christian education in mind.

Home schooling books include: *School Proof* by Mary Pride, $8.99; *All the Way Home* by Mary Pride, $13.99; *The Hows & Whys of Home Schooling* by Ray Ballman, $10.99; and *A Survivor's Guide to Home Schooling* by Shackelford and White, $8.95.

American Montessori Consulting, 11961 Wallingsford

Rd, PO Box 5062, Rossmoor CA 90720. (310) 598-2321. Email: amonco@aol.com Internet site: http://members.aol.com/amonco/amonco.html For parents who wish to incorporate Montessori teaching methods at home, this company has just the answer. They have two publications: *Modern Montessori at Home: A Creative Teaching Guide for Parents of Children Six through Nine Years of Age,* $13.95 and *Modern Montessori at Home II: A Creative Teaching Guide for Parents of Children 10 through 12 Years of Age,* $13.95.

Some of the topics covered: an introduction to the Montessori philosophy; presenting the lesson in your home; making the Montessori apparatus; and specific teaching tips.

Blue Bird Publishing, 1713 East Broadway #306, Tempe AZ 85282. (602) 968-4088, (602) 831-6063. FAX (602) 831-1829. Toll-free orders 1-800-654-1993. *Home Schools: An Alternative* by Cheryl Gorder is a homeschooling best seller that is now available in its fourth edition for $12.95. It examines the controversies of this educational alternative. The book has been widely reviewed by national magazines, including *Booklist, Small Press Book Review, GCT, Home Education Magazine,* and the *Big Book of Home Learning.* Topics covered are: the reasons parents choose homeschooling; the controversies over this alternative; the psychological, emotional, social, religious, moral, academic, historical and legal issues involved. There are also ideas for how to home school, a list of home school organizations, and lists of resources.

Parents' Guide for Helping Kids Become "A" Students, $11.95, is a practical book that teaches parents how to help their children develop better study skills. There are specific ideas for reading, math, spelling, writing, homework, memory, note-taking, and test-taking. A special feature is easy at-home activities to develop oral and communication skills. The Reading Rhinoceros bookstore owner said, "There's been an eager response on the part of parents [for this book]."
See page 176.

Bob Jones University Press, Greenville SC 29614-0001. Toll-free 1-800-845-5731. FAX toll-free 1-800-524-8398. Free home school brochure, call 1-800-739-8199. Free catalog—just call toll-free number. Their catalog contains homeschooling helps, such as the Fifth Edition of *The Home School Manual* by Ted Wade, $24.95, a homeschooling classic; and *A Survivor's Guide to Home Schooling*, which offers help in such areas as scheduling housework and teaching, coping with preschool children, choosing a curriculum, and more, $8.99.

Brook Farms Books, PO Box 246, Bridgewater ME 04735. *The Home School Source Book* by Donn Reed is actually two completely revised books combined into one. In this edition there is an emphasis on global awareness, cultural literacy, ecology, comparative religions and more, $15.00.

Christian Life Workshops (CLW), Box 2250, Gresham OR 97030. (503) 667-3942. Their catalog, *Our Family's Favorites*, has a wide variety of instructional books on how to home school. *The Original Home Schooling* a 6 volume series is just a small sample of the many guides available through their catalog.

Common Sense Press, PO Box 5863, Hollywood FL 33083. (305) 962-1930. FAX (305) 964-7644. Offers the book *How to Home School: A Practical Approach* by Gayle Graham, M.Ed. This book shows how to plan and organize a home schooling program; how to teach reading, writing, and math with ease; how to streamline record-keeping; $20. Another useful book is *How to Create Your Own Study Unit,* for showing a parent how to design an individualized study unit for the family, $16. Also, *We Home School,* a read-aloud book for kids about home schooling, $7.

Cygnet Press, Inc, HC 12, Box 7A, 116 Hwy 28, Anthony NM 88021. (505) 874-3306. *No Regrets: How Homeschooling Earned Me a Master's Degree at Age Sixteen,* the story of Alexandra Swann's homeschooling. Homeschooled, she graduated from high school at age 11, from Brigham Young University at age 15—their youngest graduate ever—and received a Master's Degree from California State University at age 16. Get this—it was all achieved through home learning. This story is not just about her, but also about the whole family of 10 children, who have been homeschooled by mother Joyce Swann.

$12.95.

Education Services, 8825 Blue Mountain Drive, Golden CO 80403. Toll-free ordering 1-800-421-6645. *You CAN Teach Your Child Successfully: Grades 4-8,* $19.

The Elijah Company, Route 2, Box 100-B, Crossville TN 38555. (615) 456-6284. FAX (615) 456-6384. Their catalog contains books to help homeschool parents, such as *The Homeschooling Father* by Michael Farris, $6.95.

FergNus Services, PO Box 578, Richlandtown PA 18955-0578. (610) 282-0401. FAX (610) 282-0402. *The Home Schooler's Journal,* is the award-winning lesson planner designed for the many ways homeschoolers really teach. There is a daily subject log for 200 days; both Julian and linear calendars; resource cost log; borrowing & lending log; objective/resource sheets; field trip logs; test scorekeeper; and library lists. All for just $7.95. They also have other homeschooling products.

Gazelle Publications, 9853 Jericho Road, Bridgman MI 49106-9742. (616) 465-4004. Toll-free 1-800-650-5076.

Email:wadeted@aol.com Publishers of *The Home School Manual,* by Ted Wade and 17 others. This book is coming into its 6th edition and is a must for homeschoolers. It takes parents from the very beginning; answering questions about legal aspects, to answering questions about specifics, like how to teach art or social studies. There are many helpful hints on teaching certain subjects, and on homeschooling in general. Especially useful are the appendices, which list everything from textbook publishers to state legal information. Editor's note: This book I keep on my own desk for reference. This book is $24.95. The *Home School Manual, Electronic Version* is 2 diskettes on Windows, $16.

Home Schooling From Scratch by Mary Potter Kenyon is Gazelle's newest book. It offers information for families who have limited resources, $10. **See ad page 107.**

Good News Publishers, Crossway Books, 1300 Crescent St., Wheaton IL 60187. FAX (708) 682-4785. Toll-free ordering 1-800-323-3890. This is one of America's favorite Christian publishers. One of their newer homeschooling titles is *The How & Why of*

Home Schooling, which gives the Biblical and empirical reasons for homeschooling, practical guidelines for successful homeschooling, and a list of resources, $9.99.

Great Christian Books, 229 South Bridge Street, PO Box 8000, Elkton MD 21922-8000. (410) 392-0930. Toll-free orders 1-800-775-5422. FAX (410) 392-3103. Email: gcb@ssnet.com Internet site: http:www.GreatChristianBooks. com Send for special catalog *Homeschool Warehouse.* Satisfaction guaranteed. This is a great one-stop shopping place for homeschooling books of all kinds!

Numerous how-to-homeschool books available in this catalog. There's *The Christian Home School* by Gregg Harris ($10.40); *Christian Home Educators Curriculum Manual* by Cathy Duffy (elementary grades or junior/ senior high, each $14.95); *Home School Seminar: Blueprint for Success* ($25.20); *How to Home School—A Practical Approach* ($16.11); and more.

Hewitt Homeschooling Resources, PO Box 9, Washougal WA 98671-0009. (360) 835-8708. FAX (360) 835-8697. This company of-fers testing services, enrollment, and unit packages. In their catalog, they also offer some home school titles, such as *Home Education Guide,* $25; Ruth Beechick's *You Can Teach Your Child Successfully,* $20; and *How to Home School* by Gayle Graham, $20.

Holt Associates, 2269 Massachusetts Ave, Cambridge MA 02140. (617) 864-3100. FAX (617) 864-9235. John Holt founded *John Holt's Bookstore,* a catalog through which he sold books about education that he thought were especially good.

Through the catalog, parents have access to these and other titles by John Holt: *How Children Fail,* $11; *How Children Learn,* $11; *Freedom and Beyond,* $15.95; *Instead of Education,* $8.95; *Never Too Late,* $9.95; *Teach Your Own,* $11.95. These are all <u>highly recommended</u> because they will explain a lot of educational background, such as how children learn, why home schooling works so effectively, the historical background and purpose of public education and why it doesn't work well.

Books specifically on homeschooling found in the catalog include: *Better Than School* by Nancy Wallace,

$10.95; *College Admissions: A Guide for Homeschoolers,* $7.95; *Hard Times in Paradise* by David & Micki Colfax, $19.95; *The Home School Source Book* by Donn Reed, $15; *Homeschooling for Excellence* by David & Micki Colfax, $9.99; the family that has homeschooled three sons who later went to Harvard, $8.95; *Famous Homeschoolers* by Malcolm Plent, 12-page brochure for $2.

Home Education Press, PO Box 1083, Tonasket WA 98855. (509) 486-1351. FAX (509) 486-2628. Toll-free ordering 1-800-236-3278. Email: HomeEdMag@aol.com Internet site: http://www.home-edpress.com Besides their *Home Education Magazine,* they have a 24-page catalog of books of interest to homeschoolers. For instance, they carry *The Home School Reader: Collected Articles from Home Education Magazine, 1984-1994;* and *I Learn Better by Teaching Myself,* an introduction to interest-initiated learning, $9.75.
See ad page 134.

Home Run Enterprises, 16172 Huxley Circle, Westminister CA 92683. (714) 841-1220. FAX (714) 841-

5584. Email: Caduffy@aol.com Cathy Duffy's book *Christian Home Educators' Curriculum Manual* has two editions, one for elementary grades, and one for high school. She reviews thousands of products for Christian homeschoolers.

Homeschool Publishing House/ Homeschool Seller, PO Box 19, Cherry Valley MA 01611-0019, (508) 791-8332. FAX (508) 791-8165. Email: HSSeller@aol.com
This home-based business has a homeschool planner called *The Abundant Blessings Homeschool Planner* (with binder, $21, without binder, $15) which conveniently keeps—for up to 8 kids— all your daily lesson plans, library lists, tests and attendance records, health records, curriculum records, field trips, and more. Refill pages and expansion pages available.
Also available is *Answers to the Tough Questions,* a booklet offering simple answers to the difficult questions most often asked about homeschooling, $4.

ICER Press Bookstore, PO Box 877, Claremount CA 91711. *School At Home* by Ingeborg U.V. Kendall is a clearly written book about homeschooling. The author brings international experience to her book since she has homeschooled her children in Switzerland and South Africa as well as the United States.

Lifetime Books & Gifts, 3900 Chalet Suzanne Dr., Lake Wales FL 33853. (941) 676-6311. Toll Free for ordering 1-800-377-0390. From their *The Always Incomplete Resource Guide & Catalog,* ($3) they offer a host of quality educational materials. It has numerous instructional material on how to home school, such as *How to Home School: A Practical Approach,* and *How to Tutor* are just two of the many books available.

The Moore Foundation, Box 1, Camas WA 98607. Raymond and Dorothy Moore have been called the "grandparents" of modern homeschooling. They are the authors of two classic homeschooling books: *Home Grown Kids, School Can Wait* and *Homeschool Burnout.* They are also the authors of other several other publications and articles for home management. They continue to conduct research and workshops internationally.

Mountain House Press, Box 353, Philo CA 95466. *Homeschooling for Excellence: How to take charge of your child's education—and why you absolutely must is* about the Colfax's family experience with homeschooling. This family is nationally known for teaching their children at home so well that the children went on to schools like Harvard. They have appeared on the *Today Show, Nightline, Good Morning America,* and more. $10.95. Their new title is *Hard Times in Paradise: An American family's struggle to carve out a homestead in California's redwood mountains,* about their life on their land, the difficulties and the triumphs. "Engrossing, fascinating."— *People Magazine.* "Their engaging story of pioneering is made all the more remarkable by the self-sufficiency of the children who were educated at home."—*Publishers Weekly.* $19.95. Author-signed copies of each of these books are available by ordering directly from Mountain Meadow Press.

Mountain Meadow Press, PO Box 447, Kooskia ID 83539. (208) 926-7875. Publishers of *Home Schooling: Taking the First Step,* revised edition, by

Borg Hendrickson. This comprehensive guide (about 330 pages) which presents in step-by-step fashion all aspects, including legal summaries for each state, and answers to home homeschoolers' questions, effective teaching practices, readings, and resources $16.95. They also have another excellent resource, *How to Write a Low Cost/ No-Cost Curriculum For Your Home School Child* by Borg Hendrickson, $14.95, which is highly recommended by many homeschool reviewers, such as *Home Education Magazine, Christian Home Educators' Curriculum Manual,* PA Homeschoolers, and more.

Parable Publishing, RD 2 Box 2002, Middlebury VT 05753. *Child Training & the Home School* by Jeff & Marge Barth, parents of 5 children and grandparents of 2, speak from years of experience in this 176-page book full of practical advice, $6.

Paradigm Company, Box 45161, Boise ID 83711. (208) 322-4440. *How to Tutor: For Parents and Teachers—A Manual That Works,* by Samuel L. Blumenfeld, is a complete instructional program. He recommends that parents start tutoring their children early as a preventative measure to ensure their educational success. This book is also an effective training tool for homeschooling parents, $19.95.

Prufrock Press™, PO Box 8813, Waco TX 76714-8813. (817) 756-3337. FAX (817) 756-3339. Toll-free ordering 1-800-998-2208. Toll-free FAX for ordering 1-800-240-0333. Internet site: http://www.purfrock.com

This company has a catalog of creative teaching ideas, including items to help teach gifted students.

Summer Island Press, PO Box 279, Williamsburg MI 49690. Publishers of *Super Student—Happy Kid!* by Sally Ketchum ($9.95), which is a practical student success guide for everyone. There are 40 chapters and over 500 tips that build self-esteem, character, confidence, and real skills.

Sycamore Tree, 2179 Meyer Place, Costa Mesa CA 92627. (714) 650-4466 for information about products and services. For ordering, call or FAX toll-free 1-800-779-6750. Internet site: http://www.sycamoretree.com/home.html

In addition to full curriculums, The Sycamore Tree offers individual materials in their comprehensive 112-page catalog. There's a wide selection of over 3,000 items. The catalog is free if you mention this book. How-to-homeschool books include Mary Pride's *The Big Book of Home Learning;* Ted Wade's *The Home School Manual; Teaching Children: A Curriculum Guide to What Children Need to Know Through 6th Grade,* and more.

See ad page 106.

TEACH Services, Donivan Road, Route 1, Box 182, Brushton NY 12916-9738. (518) 358-2125. Toll-free 1-800-367-1844. FAX (518) 358-3028. This company has a catalog of books for homeschoolers and parents. Books for teaching how-to-homeschool include: Ted Wade's classic, *Home School Manual,* 5th edition, $19.95 or 6th edition, $24.95.

Chapter Ten

HELP FOR THE HANDICAPPED
OR GIFTED STUDENT

Alexander Graham Bell Association for the Deaf Inc., 3417 Volta Place NW, Washington D.C. 20007-2778. Provides both services and support for adults and children who are deaf or hard of hearing. Teaches how to use and maintain hearing aids; reports On developments of interest; members receive regular updates on legislation. Publications for members are: *The Volta Review, and Volta Voices.* Conferences, workshops, and training are available through the organization as well as scholarships and awards. A comprehensive catalog of books computer software, curriculum, and reference materials are available.

Alliance for Parental Involvement in Education, Inc., PO Box 59, East Chatham NY 12060-0059. (518) 392-6900. Email: allpie@taconic.net Internet site: http://www.croton.com/allpie/ This is a parent-to-parent grassroots organization which assists people who wish to be involved in their children's education—whether that education takes place in public school, in private school, or at home.

The organization publishes pamphlets, a newsletter, a book catalog, and holds workshops, seminars and conferences. One of the pamphlets is on Special Education. Their book catalog has books for special education: *The Magic Feather: The Truth About Special Education,* shows how one family's boy was mistested, mislabeled, and more, but has a happy ending, $9.95; *To a Different Drumbeat: A Practical Guide to Parenting Children with Special Needs*, $16.95.

Other titles include: *How to Write an IEP*— when a child is identified as handicapped, Public Law 94-192, comes into play and an Individualized Education Program must be developed, and this book shows how, $10; *Unicorns are Real: A Right-Brained Approach to Learning* is this author's explanation of how she feels that today's schools use an overabundance of left brain methods and those with right-brain strengths are handicapped by this approach, $12.95.

American Foundation for the Blind, 11 Penn Plaza, Suite 300, New York NY 10001-2018. (212) 620-2000. TDD (212) 620-2158. They work to improve the standards of living for the blind and visually impaired people. Provides direct assistance and referral services in partnership with over 700 agencies, as well as schools, senior centers, and businesses. Regional offices in Atlanta, Chicago, Dallas, San Francisco, and Washington DC. Besides public information, the organization publishes books, has a technology center where research and development are based.

Their extensive library is one of the largest collections of printed materials on blindness in the world. This collection is accessible to blind people through the use of computerized reading machines and closed circuit television devices. The Helen Keller Archives are stored with this organization. They also record talking books. There are local, regional and national conferences. Scholarships are available to researchers.

American Speech-Language-Hearing Association, 10801 Rockville Pike, Rockville MD 20852. Toll free voice/TDD 1-800-638-8255. This is a national professional and scientific association for speech-language pathologists and audiologists. ASHA helpline 1-800-638-8255 provides free information on speech, language, and hearing disorders. Referrals are provided for speech-language pathologists and audiologists nationwide.

At Our Own Pace, 102 Willow Drive., Waukegan IL 60087. This is a new 4-page newsletter for homeschooling families with special needs.

Autism Research Institute, 4182 Adams Avenue, San Diego CA 92116. Information about autism and similar disorders, referral services for parents seeking professionals knowledgeable about autism. Has a data bank of over 23,000 detailed case histories of autistic children from 60 countries. Publishes *Autism Research Review International,* a quarterly newsletter containing brief, easy-to-read summaries of research on autism throughout the world. Subscription $18 a year. Free sample copy. Also has a publication list of numerous articles, books, films, and videotapes about autism and similar disorders.

Children's Small Press Collection, 719 N. Fourth Ave., Ann Arbor MI. 48104. (313) 668-8056. Toll-free 1-800-221-8056. Their catalog has hard to find, well-chosen books and music for tots to teens, and also resources for parents, teachers, and family support professionals.

Good reading books about the handicapped from this catalog are: *Through Her Eyes: A True Story of Love, Miracles & Realities by Linda Rivers,* about a girl who lived fully her 14 years with inspiration about positive thinking and fulfilling those dreams; proceeds from book go to Lions Sign &/or Eyebanking programs, $7.95; *Julia, Mungo & the Earthquake: A Story for Young People About Epilepsy,* an adventure about a young lady with epilepsy who saves the day at her school during an earthquake. "This is a book that delights and teaches at the same time. It will be enormously helpful in increasing the understanding of children with handicaps & it will provide inspiration and encouragement to the children who suffer from them." —Nancy Andreasen, professor of psychiatry, $7.95.

Council for Exceptional Children, 1920 Association Drive, Reston VA 22091-1589. Toll-free 1-800-CEC-READ (232-7323). TTY: (703) 264-9446. FAX (703) 264-1637.Email: cecpubs@cec.sped.org This organization has a catalog of materials to help work with and educate special children. Many of the books are geared for teachers, but there are also materials useful for parents.

There's a video package available on ADD. This package contains 4 programs: Characteristics of ADD; Instructional Strategies for ADD;

Medical Interventions for ADD; and Parenting Strategies for ADD. This set is $195. A book on the subject is *Teaching Strategies: Education of Children with Attention Deficit Disorder,* $8.90.

For the gifted student, there's *Planning Effective Curriculum for Gifted Learners,* ($29.95) which answers a often asked questions by homeschoolers—How do I plan materials for my gifted child?

Journals by this organization are: *Teaching Exceptional Children,* six times a year, $58; *Exceptional Children,* 4 times a year, $58; *Exceptional Children Education Resources,* quarterly, $89.

Cuisenaire Company, 10 Bank St., White Plains NY 10606-5026. Toll-free 1-800-237-3142. Cuisenaire rods are almost classics now, as manipulatives for learning math. Now the Cuisenaire Company has grown greatly, and their catalog offers a wide array of products, most of which are materials for learning math and science. Many of their materials are very helpful for children with special needs.

Their catalog includes educational math computer software, such as *Unifix Software*™ : *Access to Math.* This software is designed for preschool and early elementary grades and allows many children with special needs to access math manipulatives. Menus are in English and Spanish. Requires Macintosh System 7.0 or later, 3 mg RAM, $79.95.

Satisfaction guaranteed. Request a copy of their full-color 140-page catalog.

Cystic Fibrosis Foundation, 6931 Arlington Road, Bethesda MD 20814. (301) 951-4422. 1-800-FIGHT CF. Since 1955, this foundation has been working to help people with cystic fibrosis. It is a voluntary, nonprofit health organization that raises money to encourage and fund the innovative research that has already brought advances toward finding a cure for the disease. Foundation programs are research, care centers, and professional training. Publishes *Commitment,* a newsletter, three times a year, which is provided free upon request.

Free Spirit Publishing, Inc., 400 1st Avenue North Ste. 616, Minneapolis MN 55401. (612) 338-2068. FAX (612) 337-5050. *The Gifted Kids Survival Guide (For Ages 10 & Under)* and *The Gifted Kids Survival Guide (For Ages 11-18)* are books that explain what it's like to be a gifted kid and how to make life more exciting and challenging for them. They're written for the kids, but worth the effort for parents to read as well.

They also have a book *How to Reach and Teach ADD/ADHD Children,* $27.95; and *When Your Child Has LD: A Survival Guide for Parents,* $12.95.

Front Row Experience, 540 Discovery Bay Blvd., Byron CA 94514-9454. (510) 634-5710. They have a catalog of curriculums, guidebooks and materials for movement education and special education. *Are You Listening / ADD* is a handbook that contains much-needed information about ADD and overactivity, 254 pages, $16.

Hewitt Homeschooling Resources, PO Box 9, Washougal WA 98671-0009. (360) 835-8708. FAX (360) 835-8697. This company offers testing services, enrollment, and unit packages. The basic family registration is $25, then the units for a special needs package are $90 per quarter. The package includes

initial evaluation, written and phone help for curriculum suggestions, counseling, and two evaluations.

Incentive Publications, 3835 Cleghorn Ave., Nashville TN 37215-2532. (615) 385-2934. FAX (615) 385-2967. Toll-free 1-800-421-2830. Incentive Publications has two titles for students with special needs. *Something Special* (200 pages, $14.95) contains reading activities. The book begins with a section to help determine the child's skill level. The chapters contain skills-based units on three levels of difficulty. *Special Kids's Stuff,* Revised Edition (240 pages, $16.95) works on four areas—word recognition, comprehension, work study skills, and enrichment. The activities are high interest, but low vocabulary levels, to help the student achieve a level that makes him feel successful.

Learning disAbilities Resources, PO Box 716, Bryn Mawr, PA 19010. (610) 525-8336. Toll Free 1-800-869-8336. Produces and distributes educational and motivational materials for children and adults with learning problems. Materials include reading, spelling, math books and videos. For example, there's *Tic*

Tac Toe Math, a totally different way to learn math by using a series of grids. For this system, there's an instructional guide ($15.95), workbooks I, II and III ($4.50-$4.75 each), and videos to accompany the series ($18-$19.95 each).

There's a series of video tapes ($15 each) that have been filmed of Dr. Richard Cooper's presentations on learning disabilities for parents & teachers: *Problems with Social Skills; Teaching Math; Identifying Learning Problems;* and more.

Lifetime Books & Gifts, 3900 Chalet Suzanne Dr., Lake Wales FL 33853. (941) 676-6311. Toll Free for ordering 1-800-377-0390. From their *The Always Incomplete Resource Guide & Catalog,* ($3) they offer a host of quality educational materials. They carry the book *Learning Disabled Children: Ways Parents Can Help,* by Stevens.

March of Dimes, Birth Defects Foundation, National Headquarters, 1275 Mamaroneck Ave., White Plains NY 10605. (914) 428-7100. Toll-free 1-800-367-6630. The March of Dimes' purpose is to improve the health of babies by preventing birth defects and infant mortality. There are 104 chapters nationwide, and a network of volunteers from the medical, nursing, and scientific communities assist with the professional and public health agenda of the Foundation.

They have a *Catalog of Health Education Materials* which lists publications, educational kits, and audio-visual materials of interest in the areas of prenatal care, environmental hazards, teenage pregnancy, and genetics. You can call 1-800-367-6630 for this catalog, or call your nearest March of Dimes chapter.

Muscular Dystrophy Association, 114 Old Country Road, Suite 116, Mineola NY 11501. (718) 793-1100. This group supports scientific investigation seeking the causes and effective treatments for muscular dystrophy and related neuromuscular disorders. They also sponsor a broad program of selected patient and community services in addition to research, including 240 clinics nationwide for diagnostic, therapeutic, and rehabilitation services. Genetic and social service counseling available. MDA provides assistance in obtaining orthopedic appliances and daily living aids; physical and occupational therapy; flu shots; educational and recreational activities, such as summer camp for kids.

They publish the *MDA Newsmagazine* quarterly. Also publish many helpful pamphlets. Write for publications list.

National Easter Seal Society, 230 West Monroe Street, Suite 1800, Chicago IL 60606. (312) 726-6200. FAX (312) 726-1494. The Easter Seal Society serves persons with disabilities and their families, and has been doing so for 68 years. More than one million people a year benefit from quality services provided by this organization, and surveys have shown that a very high percentage rate (93%) of all Easter Seal dollars go directly to client services.

The types of disabilities served are: learning or developmental disorders; social/psychological disorders; neurological/neuromuscular disorders; orthopedic disorders; and communicative disorders. Professional education, training, public health education, and research are supported. There are over 200 local chapters.

The Easter Seal Society has a publications list on: accessibility, attitudes, awareness, dental care, independent living, safety, computer software, speech, language, hearing, stroke, and more. Order the catalog from the national office listed above or call your local chapter.

National Federation of the Blind, 1800 Johnson Street, Baltimore MD 21230. (410) 659-9314. The largest organization of the blind in the US. This organization has state and local chapters. Each year there is a national convention. The ultimate purpose of the organization is the complete integration of the blind into society on a basis of equality. Removal of legal, economic, and social discrimination is a major objective. Public education through speeches, pamphlets, radio, and TV appearances is another one of this organization's services.

They also help with assistance given to blind persons who have been discriminated against and helps blind students by awarding scholarships. The Student Division of the National Federation of the Blind exists to gain and maintain the equal educational opportunities for the blind.

A catalog is available on numerous articles and publicity materials.

Orton Dyslexia Society, Chester Building #382, 8600 LaSalle Road, Baltimore MD 21286. (410) 296-0232. This organization is concerned with specific language difficulty or developmental dyslexia. They aim to improve understanding about the disorder, promote research, share knowledge, and encourage appropriate teaching. There is a quarterly newsletter, a yearly scholarly journal, and conferences. Free publication list available.

Pioneer Productions, PO Box 328, Young AZ 85554. This organization publishes a 61 page book (plus an appendix) called, *How to Identify Your Child's Learning Problems and What to Do About Them,* by school psychologist Duane A. Gagnon. This resource helps parents identify a possible learning problem and informs parents what they can do about them. To order send $12.00 plus $2.00 for shipping to the above address.

Prufrock Press™, PO Box 8813, Waco TX 76714-8813. (817) 756-3337. FAX (817) 756-3339. Toll-free ordering 1-800-998-2208. Toll-free FAX for ordering 1-800-240-0333. Internet site: http://www.purfrock.com

This company has a catalog of creative teaching ideas, including items to help teach gifted students. *The Gifted Kid's Survival Guide Series* (there's a volume for ages 6-10, and two volumes for ages 11-18, $14.95 each); these books are classics full of valuable information for both kids and parents.

Chapter Eleven
HOME BUSINESSES

Home schooling and home business go hand-in-hand because parents who are spending time in the home with their children still require income, and a home business or a home office is the ideal way to go. Self-sufficiency fits very well with the whole philosophy behind home schooling.

Blue Bird Publishing, 1713 East Broadway #306, Tempe AZ 85282. (602) 968-4088, (602) 831-6063. FAX (602) 831-1829. The *Home Business Resource Guide,* $11.95, is a guide to information to help start a home business and to find products for home businesses. Includes: books, courses, wholesale products, newsletters & magazines, equipment & supplies. *Families Together* said, "Here at last is a book filled with vital information and sources for the Home Entrepreneur." *Book Reader* said, "An enormous amount of information put together with care.
See page 176.

Bluestocking Press, PO Box 2030, Shingle Springs CA 95682-2030. (916) 621-1123. Toll-free 1-800-959-8586. FAX (916) 642-9222. Check Bluestocking's catalog ($3) for a whole section of entrepreneurship books, such as: *The Work-at-Home Sourcebook: Over 1,000 Job Opportunities Plus Home Business Opportunities & Other Options* by Lynie Arden, 279 pages, $19.95; *Running a One-Person*

Business, $14; *Guerrilla Marketing Online,* $12.95; *Working From Home: Everything You Need,* $15.95.

For kids, there is *Better Than a Lemonade Stand,* written by a 15-year-old entrepreneur, shows kids how to earn their own money, ages 9+, $7.95. **See ad page 27.**

Center for Self Sufficiency, PO Box 416, Denver CO 80201-0416. (303) 575-5676. *Small Business Possibility Encyclopedia—World Mapping Edition,* $149.

Children's Small Press Collection, 719 N. Fourth Ave., Ann Arbor MI 48104. (313) 668-8056. Toll-free 1-800-221-8056. Their catalog has hard to find, well-chosen books and music for tots to teens, and also resources for parents, teachers, and family support professionals.

Home business book for kids from this catalog: *Better Than a Lemonade Stand: Small Business Ideas for Kids* by a 15-year-old author, $8.95.

Christian Life Workshops (CLW), Box 2250, Gresham OR 97030. (503) 667-3942. From their catalog, *Our Family's Favorites* they offer

books like *Homemade Money,* which is not a totally Christian-based book, and *Business by the Book,* which is a business book based on Christian principles.

Discovery Toys, Inc., 6400 Brisa St., Livermore CA 94550. (510) 606-2600. FAX (510) 447-0626. Toll-free 1-800-426-4777. This company sells carefully selected toys, books, and games of high quality and developmental value. Their products are distributed through nationwide network of 40,000 trained independent Educational Consultants. For a free catalog and referral to a representative in your area, call toll-free 1-800-426-4777. You can become one of these consultants—full-time or part-time. Call or write for information.

The Doula, PO Box 71, Santa Cruz CA 95063-0071. Phone/FAX (408) 464-9488. The title of the magazine is *The Doula:,* from the word "doula," a Greek word meaning "to serve" and it has come to represent women who through history "mother the new mother." The magazine nurtures and empowers women in mothering their own children. It challenges current social/

technological attitudes, viewing mothering as a vitally important commitment: encompassing pregnancy, birth, breast-feeding, midwifery, homeschooling, and health. This magazine is a good source to find current home businesses and to advertise a home business. Special subscription rate is $15 per year, 4 issues.

The Family Store, 330 McEnery Road., Felton CA 95018. This is a mail order catalog comprised of products made entirely by home or family businesses. Every dollar spent at the Family Store goes to encourage a family to work together. If your family is interested in selling items, ask for the *Seller's Prospect Sheet.*

Great Christian Books, 229 South Bridge Street, PO Box 8000, Elkton MD 21922-8000. (410) 392-0930. Toll-free orders 1-800-775-5422. FAX (410) 392-3103. Email: gcb@ssnet.com Internet site: http:www.GreatChristianBooks. com Send for special catalog *Homeschool Warehouse.* Satisfaction guaranteed. This is a great one-stop shopping place for homeschooling books of all kinds!

Two home business products available from this catalog are *Home Business Resource Guide,* $10.24; and the *Home & Family Business Workshop,* a 7-cassette tape set with complete notes by Gregg Harris, $39.99.

Illinois Christian Home Educators, PO Box 261, Zion Ill 60099. Home businesses have a special place to exhibit their products at the annual Illinois State Convention of Christian Home Educators.

Mothers Resource Guide, PO Box 469, Fallston MD 21047. (410) 877-0692. Publishes the *Mothers Resource Guide* that contains support groups for mothering. This group is also interested in home education and home businesses. There is a directory of home businesses and special ads for home businesses.

Usborne Books at Home, 10302 E. 55th Pl., Tulsa OK. (918) 622-4522 Toll-free 1-800-611-1655. They offer a book-selling opportunity for those who would like to run a business out of their home.

Chapter Twelve

HOME SCHOOL SUPPORT GROUPS

Home school support groups are a very important source of information for parents interested in home education. When I talk about home schooling on radio stations, I always suggest that the first step for a parent interested in home schooling is to contact a local support group. The group can give valuable information about how home school laws are being applied in their area, ideas about teaching, leads on resources or used materials, and some even have a library for exchanging home school materials.

You may find groups through other sources. Christian groups are listed in *The Teaching Home*. A state organization will usually have information about smaller chapters in specific areas.

There are several groups that are listed under "National" which can be very useful, but there is no one specific umbrella organization that covers all home schoolers.

This chapter lists national groups first, then state groups alphabetically by state. Include a self-addressed stamped envelope when writing to these organizations, and be as specific as possible when requesting information.

National

Alliance for Parental Involvement in Education, Inc., PO Box 59, East Chatham NY 12060-0059. (518) 392-6900. Email: allpie@taconic.net Internet site: http://www.croton.com/allpie/ This is a parent-to-parent grassroots organization which assists people who wish to be involved in their children's education—whether that education takes place in public school, in private school, or at home.

The organization publishes pamphlets, a newsletter, a book catalog, and holds workshops, seminars and conferences.

Christian Life Workshops (CLW), Box 2250, Gresham OR 97030. (503) 667-3942. This organization is a national organization with chapters across the United States and some in Great Britain. Their magazine/catalog offers a wide variety of materials to order and articles to read.

HCL, PO Box 4643, Whittier CA 90607. (310) 696-4696. This is not a support group, but rather an administrative unit serving families in California and nationwide. This organization provides standard private school services such as transferring of records, maintenance of cumulative files, course of study requirements and educational resource recommendations. It also offers a high school diploma program.

Holt Associates, 2269 Massachusetts Ave, Cambridge MA 02140. (617) 864-3100. FAX (617) 864-9235. John Holt is considered the father of modern homeschooling. If you're reading this book, you've no doubt heard much about him. He authored ten books about education including the classic, *How Children Fail.* In 1977 he founded *Growing Without Schooling,* a magazine dedicated to supporting home educators. He also founded *John Holt's Bookstore,* a catalog through which he sold books about education that he thought were especially good.

This organization is not a local homeschool support group, but rather an organization that supports homeschooling nationally. **See page 36.**

Homeschooling Information Clearinghouse, PO Box 293023, Sacramento CA 95829-3023. (916) 422-2879. Email: hicnews@aol.com This organization works to increase public understanding of and support for homeschooling by distributing information about homeschooling movement to news media, government officials, and the public. They publish a quarterly newsletter, *Spotlight*, focusing on practical ideas and advice for presenting information about homeschooling to the public.

National Center for Home Education, PO Box 159, Paeonian Springs VA 22129. (703) 338-7600. FAX (703) 338-2733. The Center was founded by the Home School Legal Defense Association to serve state leaders by informing them of homeschool legislation on a monthly basis. State organizations can request information from them without charge.

National Home Education Research Institute, ATTN. Dr. Brian Ray Western Baptist College 5000 Deer Park Dr. SE, Salem OR 97301-9392. (503) 375-7019. Email: bray@wbc.edu This organization, founded by Dr. Brian Ray, produces quality research on home education, and serves as a clearinghouse of research for home educators, researchers, and policymakers. They have a video, *What Research Says About Home Schooling*, ($24) that describes the facts concerning homeschooling. They have been publishing the quarterly academic research journal, *Home School Researcher.* The publication is $25 a year.

ALABAMA

Christian Home Education Fellowship of Alabama, PO Box 563, Alabaster AL 35007. (205) 664-2232.

ALASKA

Alaska Private & Home Education Association (APHEA), PO Box 141764, Anchorage AK 99514. (907) 696-0641. Publishes a newsletter and hosts events.

ARIZONA

Arizona Families for Home Education, PO Box 4661, Scottsdale AZ 85161-4661. (602) 941-3938. Membership in this organization ($25 family) includes: information packet notes on Arizona homeschooling laws and lists of resources, research and voting information, free curriculum fair and convention admission. The annual Home Educator's Convention and Curriculum Fair is held in May or June.

Christian Home Educators of Arizona (CHEA), PO Box 13445, Scottsdale AZ 85267-3445.

Flagstaff Home Educators, 6910 West Suzette Lane, Flagstaff AZ 86001-8220. (520) 774-0806.

ARKANSAS

Arkansas Christian Home Education Association, Box 4410, North Little Rock AR 72116. (501) 758-9099.

CALIFORNIA

California Home Educators, 10489 Sunland Blvd., PO Box 4070, Sunland CA 91040. (818) 898-0180. Toll-free 1-800-525-4419. FAX (818) 951-5963.Email: aq483@lafn. org This support group holds an annual curriculum convention. They also have a quarterly homeschooling publication, *Educating Our Children.* They offer legal defense membership for $25 per family per year, have a home school radio broadcast, and have other administrative services for Independent Study Programs.

Christian Home Educator's Association, PO Box 2009. Norwalk, CA 90651-2009.

(310) 864-3747. Toll-free 1-800-564-CHEA. Publish the magazine, *The Parent Educator Magazine* for members.

Home School Association of California, PO Box 2442, Atascadero CA 93423. Founded in 1987 as the Northern California Homeschool Association, this organization supports and promotes homeschooling by providing information, monitoring legislation, and conducting an annual convention in Sacramento.

Sacramento Council of Parent Educators (SCOPE), PO Box 163178, Sacramento CA 95816. Phone or FAX (916) 368-0401. This support group offers the newsletter, *Scope News*, meetings, work shops, curriculum fairs, speakers, library, and advertises for businesses that have a Christian or homeschooling focus. SCOPE subscribers are able to take advantage of the SCOPE library which offers books, software, videos and audio materials.

COLORADO

Christian Home Educators of Colorado, 1015 S. Gaylord St. #226, Denver CO 80209. (303) 388-1888. (303) 777-

1022. This is a support group that has an annual convention, a quarterly newsletter, a resource list, a support group directory, and information on Colorado Home School Law. Volunteers and donations are welcome.

CONNECTICUT

Education Association of Christian Homeschoolers, 25 Fieldstone Run, Farmington CT 06032.

DELAWARE

Delaware Home Education Association, 11 Bristol Knoll Rd., Newark, DE 19711. (302) 633-8528 FAX (302) 993-5950. They publish *Tri-State Network Newsletter.*

Tri-State Home School Network, PO Box 7193, Newark DE 19714. (302) 368-4217.

DISTRICT OF COLUMBIA

Boiling Area Home Schoolers of D.C., 1516 E Carswell Circle, Washington DC 20036.

FLORIDA

Florida Parent-Educators Association, 3781 SW 18th St., Ft. Lauderdale FL 33312. (407) 723-1714.

GEORGIA

Georgia Home Education Association, 245 Buckeye Lane, Fayetteville GA 30214. (404) 461-3657.

North Georgia Home Education Association, 200 West Crest Road, Rossville GA 30741.

HAWAII

Christian Homeschoolers of Hawaii, 91-824 Oama St., Ewa Beach HI 96706. (808) 689-6398.

IDAHO

Idaho Home Educators, Box 4022, Boise ID 83711-4022. (208) 482-7336. This group has a June curriculum swap and a spring curriculum workshop. The group publishes *The Bulletin* that pertains to news for home educators of southwestern Idaho.

ILLINOIS

Christian Home Educators Coalition, Box 470322, Chicago IL 60647. (312) 278-0673.

Illinois Christian Home Educators, PO Box 261, Zion Ill 60099. (708) 662-0230. Annual Illinois State Convention of Christian Home Educators. This convention also has exhibitors from cottage industries.

INDIANA

Fort Wayne Area Home Schools, PO Box 12954, Fort Wayne IN 46866-2954. (219) 483-2807. A support group that sponsors an annual curriculum fair.

Indiana Association of Home Educators, 1000 N. Madison, Suite S2, Greenwood IN 46142. (317) 770-0644.

IOWA

Network of Iowa Christian Home Educators, Box 158, Dexter IA 50070. (515) 789-4310 or toll-free 1-800-723-0438.

KANSAS

Christian Home Education Confederation of Kansas, PO Box 3564, Shawnee Mission KS 66203. (316) 945-0810.

Teaching Parents Associa- **tion,** 100 East 109th St. North, Valley Center KS 67147. This Wichita-area organization has an annual Home School Workshop in the spring. The workshop includes speakers, seminars, and exhibits.

KENTUCKY

Christian Home Educators of Kentucky, 691 Howardstown Road, Hodgenville KY 42748. (502) 358-9270. Annual home school convention in Louisville, KY.

Kentucky Home Education Association, PO Box 81, Winchester KY 40392-0081. (606) 744-8562.

LOUISIANA

Christian Home Educators Fellowship of Louisiana (CHEF), PO Box 74292, Baton Rouge LA 70784-4292. (504) 775-9709. Holds a homeschool convention and book fair with nationally known speakers. Getting Started Packet $10.

MAINE

Homeschoolers of Maine, HC 62 Box 24, Hope ME 04847. (207) 763-4251. Is a local support group for Maine residents.

MARYLAND

Christian Home Educators Network, 304 N. Beechwood Ave., Catonsville MD 21228. (410) 744-8919. (410) 444-5465.

Maryland Association of Christian Home Education Organizations, PO Box 3964, Frederick MD 21705. (301) 663-3999.

MASSACHUSETTS

Massachusetts Homeschool Organization of Parent Educators, 15 Ohio St., Wilmington MA 01887. (508) 658-8970. Annual convention and legislative action.

MICHIGAN

Great Lakes Christian Educators' Convention, 8585 Dixie Hwy, Clarkston MI 48348. (810) 625-2311. Support groups that hold an annual Great Lakes Christian Educators' Convention with participating states of Michigan, Ohio, Illinois, Indiana and Wisconsin.

Home School Support Network of Michigan, PO Box 2457, Riverview MI 48192. (313) 284-1249. This organization works to encourage and equip parents in educating their own children. They provide information through their newspaper, *Home Educators' Family Times,* and hold an annual Detroit Regional Home Education Conference which has a curriculum fair, a used book sale, and training workshops.

Information Network for Christian Homes, 4934 Cannonsburg Road, Belmont MI 49306. (616) 874-5656.

MINNESOTA

Minnesota Association of Christian Home Educators, (MACHE), PO Box 32308, Fridley MN 55432-0308. (612) 717-9070. This group has an annual curriculum fair and convention in the spring in the St. Paul Civic Center, St. Paul, MN. There are almost 800 active members.

MISSISSIPPI

Mississippi Home Educators Association, Route 9, Box 350, Laurel MS 39440. (601) 649-MHEA.

MISSOURI

Families for Home Education, 400 E. High Point Lane, Columbia MO 65203. (816) 826-9302.

Missouri Association of Christian Teaching Homes, 307 E. Ash St., #146, Columbia MO 65201. (314) 443-8217.

MONTANA

Montana Coalition of Home Schools, PO Box 654, Helena MT 59624. (406) 587-6163.

NEVADA

Home Schools United—Vegas Valley, PO Box 93564, Las Vegas NY 89193. (702) 870-9566.

Northern Nevada Home Schools, Inc., c/o Connie Packer, 4010 DeSoto Way, Reno NV 89502.

Northern Nevada Home Schools, PO Box 21323, Reno NV 89515. (702) 852-6647.

NEW HAMPSHIRE

Christian Home Educators of New Hampshire, PO Box 961, Manchester NH 03105.

NEW JERSEY

Education Network of Christian Homeschoolers, 120 Mayfair Lane, Mount Laurel NJ 08054. (609) 222-4823.

Unschoolers Network, 2 Smith St., Farmingdale NJ 07727. (908) 938-2473.

NEW MEXICO

New Mexico Christian Home Educators, 5749 Paradise Blvd., NW, Albuquerque MN 87114. (505) 897-1772.

NEW YORK

Loving Education at Home, PO Box 88, Cato NY 13003. (716) 346-0939.

NORTH CAROLINA

North Carolinians for Home Education, 419 N. Boylan Ave., Raleigh NC 27603. (919) 834-6243.

NORTH DAKOTA

North Dakota Home School Association, 4007 N. State St., Rt. 5, Box 9, Bismarck ND 58501. (701) 223-4080. This is a support group that holds an annual home school convention in Bismarck, North Dakota, publishes a monthly newsletter, and lobbies during the legislative session.

OHIO

Christian Home Educators of Ohio, PO Box 262, Columbus OH 43216. (614) 474-3177.

Home Education Action Council of Ohio, PO Box 24133, Huber Heights OH 45424. (513) 242-9226.

OKLAHOMA

Christian Home Educators Fellowship of Oklahoma, PO Box 471363, Tulsa OK 74147-1363. (918) 583-7323.

Oklahoma Central Home Educators Association, (OCHEC), PO Box 270601, Oklahoma City OK 73137. (405) 521-8439. Support group that holds an annual convention in Oklahoma City.

OREGON

Christian Home Education Support Services of Oregon, PO Box 13693, Portland OR 97213-0693. (503) 784-4398. Produces the Northwest Curriculum Exhibition, an annual display in Portland, Oregon, of materials that support Christian principles. Exhibitors are by invitation only.

Oregon Christian Home Education Association (OCEAN), 2515 NE 37th, Portland OR 97212. Phone/FAX (503) 288-1285. This organization gives first time information, referrals to support groups, information to group leaders, leadership training, and is politically active.

PENNSYLVANIA

Christian Home School Association of Pennsylvania, PO Box 3603, York PA 17402-0603. (717) 661-2428.

Pennsylvania Homeschoolers, RD 2 Box 117, Kittanning PA 16201. (412) 783-6512.

RHODE ISLAND

Rhode Island Guild of Home Teachers, PO Box 11, Hope RI 02831-0011. (401) 821-1546. This group sponsors an annual curriculum fair.

SOUTH CAROLINA

South Carolina Association of Independent Home Schools, PO Box 2104, Irmo

SC 29063. (803) 551-1003.

South Carolina Home Educators Association, PO Box 612, Lexington SC 29071. (803) 951-8960.

SOUTH DAKOTA

Western Dakota Christian Home Schools (WDCHS), HCR 74, Box 28, Murdo SD 57559. (605) 669-2508. This organization sponsors monthly support groups, meetings, children's activities, and publishes a monthly newsletter.

TENNESSEE

Tennessee Home Education Association, Smoky Mountain Chapter, c/o Robert and Sherry Ward, 103 Moss Road, Oak Ridge TN 37830. (615) 482-6857. Support group that holds an annual Educational Resources Fair in Knoxville, Tennessee.

TEXAS

Christian Home Education Association of Austin, PO Box 141998, Austin TX 78714-1998. (512) 450-0070. Support meetings, organization library, annual bookfair/ convention, social activities, seminars such as "How do I begin?" Newsletter *CHEA of Austin* publishes notices of meetings, announcements, and events.

Family Educators Alliance of South Texas, 4719 Blanco Rd., San Antonio TX 78212. (210) 342-4674.

Home-Oriented Private Education for Texas, PO Box 59876, Dallas TX 75229-9876. (214) 358-2221.

North Texas Home Education Network, Box 59627, Dallas TX 75229. (214) 234-2366.

Southeast Texas Home School Association, 4950 FM 1960 W., Suite C3-87, Houston TX 77069. (713) 370-8787. The service area for this homeschooling area has been broadening to include the entire Gulf Coast region of the United States. They hold an Annual Home School Conference in the summer. It is SETHA's purpose to bring praise and glory to God by providing information and support to home school families and others interested in home schooling.

Texas Home School Coalition, PO Box 6982, Lubbock

TX 79493 (806) 797-4927. Publishes a newsletter called *The Alert*, for $25.00 per year.

UTAH

Utah Christian Homeschoolers, PO Box 3942, Salt Lake City UT 84110-3942. (801) 969-9657.

Utah Home Education Association, 8439 West 3410 South, Magna UT 84044. (801) 252-1011. Support group that holds an annual convention and curriculum fair.

VERMONT

Christian Home Educators of Vermont, 2 Webster St., Barre VT 05641. (802) 476-8821.

Vermont Homeschoolers Association, c/o Jim and Mary Smith, RR 1 Box 149, Hartland VT 05048. (802) 436-3146.

VIRGINIA

B.E.A.C.H., 1305 White Marlin Lane, Virginia Beach VA 23464. (804) 474-0389. FAX (804) 579-6114. Email: dplast@exis.net Internet site: http://wwwp.exis.net/~dplast/beach.htm
This group has a Mid-

Atlantic Curriculum Fair. They publish the *Bayith Educator* newsletter.

Home Educators Association of Virginia, 1900 Byrd Avenue, Suite 201, PO Box 6745, Richmond VA 23230. (804) 288-1608. FAX (804) 288-6962. This support group has a newsletter, *The Virginia Home Educator,* (available to members and membership is $25 per year), an annual convention in Richmond, and a list of resources. One handy resource is *The Virginia Home School Manual,* available from them for $22.50 (member price).

WASHINGTON

Inland Empire Home School Center, PO Box 1750, Airway Heights WA 99001. Toll-free 1-800-378-4699. Holds educational workshops, offers student testing, tutorial, and publications. The newsletter, *Inland Empire Home School News,* has a list of Spokane area support groups, organizations and news about Washington state homeschooling.

Washington Association of Teaching Christian Homes (WATCH), N. 2904 Dora Road, Spokane WA 99212.

Yearly curriculum fair, speakers, seminars with a Christian emphasis. Has had homeschool qualifying courses. Publishes *WATCH Notes* newsletter. Pamphlet available upon request: Home School Law in the State of Washington.

Washington Homeschool Organization, 18130 Midvale Ave. N., Seattle WA 98083.

WEST VIRGINIA

Christian Home Education Association of West Virginia, PO Box 8770, South Charleston WV 25303. (304) 776-4664.

West Virginia Home Educators Association, (WVHEA), PO Box 3707, Charleston VA 25337-3707. Toll-free 1-800-736-9843 (WVHE). This group has an annual spring family day, a fall fair, a handbook, and testing services.

WISCONSIN

Wisconsin Christian Home Educators, 2307 Carmel Ave., Racine WI 53405. (414) 637-5127.

WYOMING

Homeschoolers of Wyoming, 339 Bicentennial Court, Powell WY 82435. (307) 754-3271. This group has a state newsletter, county contacts who pass on important happenings and legislative updates, a fine arts fair, and a convention.

Chapter Thirteen
HOME SCHOOL MAGAZINES & NEWSLETTERS

Alaska Private & Home Education Association (APHEA), PO Box 141764, Anchorage AK 99514. (907) 696-0641. Publishes the *APHEA Network News,* 11 months per year.

Alliance for Parental Involvement in Education, Inc., PO Box 59, East Chatham NY 12060-0059. (518) 392-6900. Email: allpie@taconic.net Internet site: http://www.croton.com/allpie/ This is a parent-to-parent grassroots organization which assists people who wish to be involved in their children's education—whether that education takes place in public school, in private school, or at home.

The organization publishes pamphlets, a newsletter, *Options in Learning,* a book catalog, and holds workshops, seminars and conferences. The pamphlets available are on Parent/ Student Rights; Special Education; Public Education; Home Education for Parents; Home Education for School Personnel; Alternative Education; Montessori, Quaker & Waldorf Education.

The organization also offers *New York State Home Education News* newsletter for the homeschool community in New York State.

B.E.A.C.H., 1305 White Marlin Lane, Virginia Beach VA 23464. (804) 474-0389. FAX (804) 579-6114. Email: dplast@exis.net Internet site: http://wwwp.exis.net/~dplast/beach.html This group holds a Mid-Atlantic Curriculum Fair. They publish the *Bayith Educator* newsletter.

California Home Educators, 10489 Sunland Blvd., PO Box 4070, Sunland CA 91040. (818) 898-0180. Toll-free 1-800-525-4419. FAX (818) 951-5963.Email: aq483@lafn.org This support group has a quarterly homeschooling publication, *Educating Our Children.*

Catholic Home School Newsletter, 688 11th Ave NW, New Brighton MN 55112. (612) 636-5761. This three-page newsletter is prepared once a year, and may be photocopied by anyone. To order an issue, send a SASE to the above address.

Christian Home Education Association of Austin, PO Box 142032, Austin TX 78714-2032. Newsletter *CHEA of Austin* publishes notices of meetings, announcements, and events.

Christian Home Educator's Association, PO Box 2009. Norwalk, CA 90651-2009. (310) 864-3747. They publish the magazine, *The Parent Educator Magazine* for members.

Christian Home Educators of Colorado, 1015 S. Gaylord St. #226, Denver CO 80209. (303) 388-1888. (303) 777-1022. This is a support group that has a quarterly newsletter, the *Homeschool Update.*

Christian Life Workshops (CLW), Box 2250, Gresham OR 97030. (503) 667-3942. *Our Family's Favorites* is the magazine/catalog that this organization publishes which offers a wide variety of Christian based material.

Delaware Home Education Association, 11 Bristol Knoll Rd, Newark, DE 19711. (302) 633-8528 FAX 302-633-8915. They publish the *Tri-State Home School Network Newsletter.*

Drinking Gourd, PO Box 2557, Redmond WA 98073. This is a *Multicultural Home Education Magazine*, published by Donna Nichols-White, started in 1992. The goal of the publication is to explore and celebrate the diversity of homeschool families.

Holt Associates, 2269 Massachusetts Ave, Cambridge MA 02140. (617) 864-3100. FAX (617) 864-9235. In 1977 John Holt founded *Growing Without Schooling,* a magazine dedicated to supporting home educators. This magazine is still available for $25 per year.

Home Education Press, PO Box 1083, Tonasket WA 98855. (509) 486-1351. FAX (509) 486-2628. Toll-free ordering 1-800-236-3278. Email: HomeEdMag@aol.com Internet site: http://www.home-edpress.com This company publishes the *Home Education Magazine.* This is an excellent well-rounded national homeschooling magazine. There is something for everyone in this publication. There are scholarly yet readable articles about parental rights, ideas on developing curriculum, learning and teaching helps, book and product reviews, marketplace ads from national products, kids pages, and more! What I especially like about this magazine is that it's for every homeschooler.
See ad page 134.

Home Educators Association of Virginia, 1900 Byrd Avenue, Suite 201, PO Box 6745, Richmond VA 23230. (804) 288-1608. FAX (804) 288-6962. This support group has a newsletter, *The Virginia Home Educator,* a 28-page quarterly that specializes in information for Virginia homeschoolers. The newsletter is available to members, and membership is $25 per year.

Homefires, 180 El Camino Real, Suite 10, Millbrae CA 94030. (415) 365-9425. The subtitle of *Homefires* is: "A joyful resource publication with ideas and activities for enhancing home education, independent study, and family fun." The publication has information about support groups, field trips, cooperative classes, workshops and events, as well as articles about education, child development, gifted children, home businesses and items of interest to homeschoolers. Subscription, $24.95, 1 year, 6 issues.

Home Life, PO Box 1250, 1731 Smizer Mill Road, Fenton MO 63026-1850. (314) 225-9790. FAX (314) 225-0743. *Practical Homeschooling* is Mary Pride's magazine for living and learning at home. This quarterly magazine has features, columns, and reviews.

Homeschoolers of Maine, HC 62 Box 24, Hope ME 04847. (207) 763-4251. Publishes the newsletter, *Heart of the Home.*

Homeschoolers of Wyoming, PO Box 926, Evansville WY 82636. (307) 237-4383. This group has a state newsletter.

Homeschooling Today, PO Box 9596, Birmingham AL 35220.

Home Schools United—Vegas Valley, PO Box 93564, Las Vegas NY 89193. (702) 870-9566. Newsletter is $15 for 12 monthly issues.

Home School Support Network of Michigan, PO Box 2457, Riverview MI 48192. (313) 284-1249. This organization publishes the *Home Educators' Family Times,* which is now mailed to almost all 50 states, but has an emphasis pertaining to conferences in the New England states, Michigan, and North Carolina.

Homeschooling Information Clearinghouse, PO Box 293023, Sacramento CA 95829-3023. (916) 422-2879. Email: hicnews@aol.com They publish a quarterly newsletter, *Spotlight,* focusing on practical ideas and advice for presenting information about homeschooling to the public.

Idaho Home Educators, Box 4022, Boise ID 83711-4022. (208) 482-7336. This group holds a June curriculum swap, and a spring curriculum workshop. The group publishes *The Bulletin* for news pertaining to

home educators of southwestern Idaho.

Inland Empire Home School Center, PO Box 1750, Airway Heights WA 99001. Toll-free 1-800-378-4699. Holds educational workshops, offers student testing, tutorial, and publications. The newsletter, *Inland Empire Home School News,* has a list of Spokane area support groups, organizations and news about Washington state homeschooling.

International Montessori Society, 912 Thayer Ave, Silver Spring MD 20910. (301) 589-1127. Publishes the *Montessori Observer,* a quarterly publication for members of the organization. The purpose of the publication is to provide news and information about the development of Montessori education to extend awareness of Montessori principles.

Massachusetts Homeschool Organization of Parent Educators, 15 Ohio St., Wilmington MA 01887. (508) 658-8970. Newsletter available.

The Moore Foundation, Box 1, Camas WA 98607. Raymond and Dorothy Moore have been called the "grandparents" of modern home-schooling. They are the authors of the classic homeschooling books: *Home Grown Kids, School Can Wait* and *Homeschool Burnout*. They are also the authors of several other publications and articles for home management. They continue to conduct research and workshops internationally. Their bimonthly publication is the *Moore Report International,* $12 per year.

Mothers Resource Guide, PO Box 469, Fallston MD 21047. (410) 877-0692. They publish a magazine-type guide that focuses on home issues. A 1 year subscription, 4 quarterly issues, is only $6.95.

National Home Education Research Institute, ATTN. Dr. Brian Ray Western Baptist College 5000 Deer Park Dr. SE, Salem OR 97301-9392. (503) 375-7019. Email: bray@wbc.edu This organization, founded by Dr. Brian Ray, produces quality research on home education, and serves as a clearinghouse of research for home educators, researchers, and policymakers. They have been publishing the quarterly academic research journal, *Home School Researcher.* The publication is $25 a year.

New Attitude, 6920 SE Hogan, Gresham OR 97080. (503) 669-1236. This is a Christian teen homeschooling magazine, started this year by 21-year-old homeschooled Josh Harris.

Sacramento Council of Parent Educators (SCOPE), PO Box 163178, Sacramento CA 95816. Phone or FAX (916) 368-0401. Publishes the newsletter, *Scope News,* which is a Christian based homeschooling newsletter. Membership subscription is 12 months for $16.00. Make checks payable to SCOPE and mail to the above address.

Shady Grove Church, 1829 W. Shady Grove Church, Grand Prairie TX 75050. (214) 790-0800. This church offers a variety of curriculum counseling, testing and newsletters. Fellowships are available.

Teaching Home, PO Box 20219, Portland OR 97294. (503) 253-9633. Subscription address and phone: PO Box 469069, Escondido CA 92046-9069. Toll-free 1-800-395-7760. *The Teaching Home* is a national Christian homeschooling magazine, published bimonthly. Its purpose is to share information and to provide support for Christian homeschooling families and organizations. Subscription is 1 year, 6 issues, $15.

Texas Home School Coalition, PO Box 6982, Lubbock TX 79493 (806) 797-4927. Publishes a newsletter called *The Alert*, for $25.00 per year.

Vermont Homeschoolers Association, c/o Natalie Casco, 80 Garron Rd, Middletown Springs, VT 05757 (802) 235-2457. Publishes a newsletter.

Washington Association of Teaching Christian Homes (WATCH), N. 2904 Dora Road, Spokane WA 99212. Yearly curriculum fair, speakers, seminars with a Christian emphasis.Homeschool qualifying courses. Publishes *WATCH Notes* newsletter. Pamphlet available upon request; *Home School Law in the State of Washington.*

Western Dakota Christian Home Schools (WDCHS), HCR 74, Box 28, Murdo SD 57559. (605) 669-2508. Publishes a monthly newsletter.

Wisdom's Gate, PO Box 125, Sawyer MI 49125. This company publishes the *Home School Digest,* now in its eighth year. This magazine emphasizes character building and family-based discipleship while addressing the deeper issues surrounding home education. Featured articles include topics such as: socialization, teenage rebellion, courtship, family-based church, field trips, dealing with learning disabilities, government involvement in education, etc. This magazine is published quarterly, (nearly 100 pages each issue) and subscription price is $18 per year. **See ad page 134.**

Chapter Fourteen

SPEAKERS, CONFERENCES
WORKSHOPS & SEMINARS

Blue Bird Publishing, 2266 S. Dobson #275, Mesa AZ 85202. (602) 831-6063. FAX (602) 831-1829. Email: bluebird @ bluebird1.com Internet site: http://www.bluebird1. com Cheryl Gorder, author of *Home Schools: An Alternative, Home Education Resource Guide, Home Business Resource Guide,* and other homeschool books, is available for speaking engagements, radio and TV shows, and workshops.

Christian Home Educator's Association, PO Box 2009. Norwalk, CA 90651-2009. (310)864-3747. Annual convention.

Christian Home Educators of Colorado, 1015 South Gaylord St. #226, Denver CO 80209. (303) 777-1022. Annual convention.

Christian Life Workshops (CLW), Box 2250, Gresham OR 97030. (503) 667-3942. Offers a full itinerary of speakers and seminars throughout the US and Great Britain. The speaker and seminar schedule is available through the catalog/magazine, *Our Family Favorites.*

Homeschoolers of Maine, HC 62 Box 24, Hope ME 04847. (207) 763-4251. Announces conferences through their newsletter, *The Heart of Home.*

Home School Legal Defense Association, PO Box 159, Paeonian Springs VA 20219. (540) 338-5600. FAX (540)

338-2733. Michael Farris, president of the organization, and J. Michael Smith, vice-president, are available to speak at homeschool conventions.

Informed Homebirth/ Informed Birth & Parenting, PO Box 3675, Ann Arbor MI 48106. (313) 662-6857. Annual conference on "The Young Child; Waldorf Principles for Early Childhood" every April.

Konos Curriculum, PO Box 1534, Richardson TX 75083. (214) 669-8337. A six-hour seminar on cassette is available to train parents how to use their Christian character curriculum. Live seminars can be scheduled for groups as well.

Landmark Distributors, PO Box 849, Fillmore CA 93015. (805) 524-3263. This is a family-owned organization that advocates the Principle Approach to American Christian Education. Basically, the Principle Approach is the ability to learn the Biblical origin of the subjects being taught. This approach develops Christian character. Alan and Lori Harris are available to conduct Landmark Workshops, which teach this approach.

The Moore Foundation, Box 1, Camas WA 98607. Raymond and Dorothy Moore have been called the "grandparents" of modern homeschooling. They are the authors of the classic homeschooling books: *Home Grown Kids, School Can Wait* and *Homeschool Burnout.* They are also the authors of several other publications and articles for home management. They continue to conduct research and workshops internationally.

Mountain House Press, Box 353, Philo CA 95466. David and Micki Colfax are available as conference speakers. You may recall that they are the authors of *Homeschooling for Excellence,* and the parents of the homeschooled children who went on to Harvard. They have appeared on numerous TV shows, such as *Good Morning America, Today Show,* and *Nightline.*

National Home Education Research Institute, ATTN. Dr. Brian Ray Western Baptist College 5000 Deer Park Dr. SE, Salem OR 97301-9392. (503) 375-7019. Email: bray@wbc.edu This organization, founded by Dr. Brian Ray, produces quality research on home education, and serves as a clearinghouse of research for home educators, researchers, and policymakers. Dr. Ray is a conference and seminar speaker on topics such as education research, science education, and family issues.

New Attitude, 6920 SE Hogan, Gresham OR 97080. (503) 669-1236. Editor 21-year-old homeschooled Josh Harris speaks at Christian homeschool conventions.

Northwest Curriculum Exhibition, 2515 NE 37th Ave, Portland OR 97212. The Northwest Curriculum Exhibition is held in Portland each summer.

Parable Publishing, RD 2 Box 2002, Middlebury VT 05753. The Barth family is available to speak at seminars and conventions.

Paradigm Company, Box 45161, Boise ID 83711. (208) 322-4440. Author Sam Blumenfeld is available to speak at seminars and conventions.

Parents' Rights, 12571 Northwinds Drive, St. Louis MO 63146. (314) 434-4171. *Parents' Rights* a quarterly newsletter is just one of the publication this active group publishes. This group also participates in legal action, hosts educational conferences, provides speakers for conferences and meetings, supports private schools, and is active in many other activities as well. A yearly subscription is $15.00 (prices include postage).

Peter Marshall Ministries, 81 Finlay Road, Orleans MA 02653. (508) 255-7705. FAX (508) 255-2062. Toll-free 1-800-879-3298. Rev. Peter Marshall is available to speak at seminars and conventions.

Chapter Fifteen
AUDIO-VISUAL MATERIALS
MUSIC EDUCATION
& MUSICAL INSTRUMENTS

Alpha Omega Publications, 300 N. McKemy Ave, Chandler AZ 85226-2618. (602) 438-2717 Toll-free 1-800-622-3070 FAX (602) 940-8924. Email:aop@home-schooling. com Internet site: http:www.home-schooling. com This company has an extensive range of products available for homeschoolers. In fact, they produce an 88-page full-color catalog! All materials are written with Christian education in mind.

The catalog contains children's videos and audios, such as *The Amazing Book Video,* a captivating animated video that teaches children about the Bible, $8.95. There are also the *Amazing Miracles Video,* $8.95 and the *Amazing*

Children Video, $8.95. Each of these is also available on audio for $5.95 each.

The Music Machine Series: Music Machine or *Benny's Biggest Battles* are audio cassettes that have enchanted many listeners, $8.95 each. More lively Christian music is available on the audio tapes *God is My Friend, God is Great, Born Again, Story of Little Tree,* and others, each $5.95.

Audio-Forum, 96 Broad St., Guilford CT 06437-2612. (203) 453-9794. FAX (203) 453-9774.Email: 74537.550 @Compuserve.com

This company has several catalogs which have audio materials: *The Whole World*

Language Catalog, which has foreign language courses; *Guilford Green Tapes,* which has a medley of audio materials, and *About Music,* which contains music education and information about composers.

Their language catalog contains 275 courses in 96 languages—the most comprehensive foreign language catalog I've ever seen. These courses were developed by the U.S. State Department's Foreign Language Service Institute for diplomats. There's every language imaginable, including Native American dialects.

Making Music with Children Volumes I and 2, is a music education series that shows how to have fun with music while developing musical skills in children, each volume $24.95.

Bend Cornerstone Books, 62570 Dixon Loop, Bend OR 97701. Toll-free 1-800-487-5952. Free catalog of Bibles, books, tapes and videos for the entire family. They specialize in reprints of literature and historical books.

Bob Jones University Press, Greenville SC 29614-0001. Toll-free 1-800-845-5731. FAX toll-free 1-800-524-8398. Free home school brochure, call 1-800-739-8199. Free catalog—just call toll-free number. They have some videos in their catalog, such as *King Lear,* the Shakespearean tragedy, 120 minutes, $19.95; *Macbeth,* 130 minutes, $29.95; and *Red Runs the River,* the story of the Battle of Bull Run, 90 minutes, $19.95.

Other videos include the *Moody Science Adventures,* which are short films designed for children in primary grades through junior high. Each video has 3 films lasting 10 minutes each and is $14.95. Topics: *The Power in Plants,* time-lapse photography of flower, hard-working bees; *The Wonder of You,* with the amazing transformation of a caterpillar into a butterfly, the amazing human body, and our sense of taste; more.,

Bornstein School of Memory Training, 11693 San Vicente Blvd., Los Angeles CA 90049. (310) 478-2056. Credit card orders toll-free 1-800-468-2058. Memory training expert Arthur Bornstein has devised unique new memory training methods. These are effective learning aids for all ages, and will help children do better in their school work! These products have been designed for math, states and capitals, spelling, and vocabulary. The systems use visual aids as well as audio cassettes. Call or write for free catalog. More information and description of products found in Chapter Three.

Builder Books, PO Box 99, Riverside WA 98849. (509) 826-6021. Toll-free orders 1-800-260-5461. Their catalog has a "Music and Art" section which lists many available materials.

Carolina Biological Supply Company, 2700 York Road., Burlington NC 27215-3398. (910) 584-0381. Toll-free 1-800-334-5551. Toll-free FAX 1-800-222-7112. Internet site: http//www.carosci.com

This company has an enormous (over 1,000 color pages!) catalog for science and math supplies. There is an unbelievable selection of everything you can imagine—from skeletons to plant tissues to butterfly displays to microscopes. You name it—they probably have it.

There are over 50 pages in the catalog devoted to audio-visual materials. Of particular interest to homeschoolers might be their video programs from *The Discovery Channel.* Most of these tapes run $19.95, such as: *Splendors*

of the Sea: The Caribbean's Secret World; Oceans of Air: The Olympic Peninsula; Spirits of the Rainforest; In Celebration of Trees.

Another interesting series is the *Eyewitness Video Series,* each $19.95 with 30 minutes of the wonders and fascination of nature. Titles: *The Jungle; Insects; Sharks; Dinosaurs; Reptiles; The Skeleton;* and more.

And if that wasn't impressive enough, there's a *National Geographic Collection,* from $14.95 to $19.95. Titles: *The Invisible World; Rain Forest; Reptiles and Amphibians; Killer Whales— Wolves of the Sea; The Grizzlies; Gorilla; Mysteries of Mankind,* and more.

Children's Small Press Collection, 719 N. Fourth Ave., Ann Arbor MI 48104. (313) 668-8056. Toll-free 1-800-221-8056. Their catalog has a section of music books with tapes, such as *Marvelous Musical Adventures: for Developing Early Musicianship* is a delightful tape with 19 activity game-songs for 2 to 6-year-olds. Tape $9.95; book $10. *Makin' Music: Playsongs & Games* is a packed with 17 participation games, songs & dances. Tape, $9.95; book $10.

Christian Life Workshops (CLW), Box 2250, Gresham OR 97030. (503) 667-3942. *The Basic Home Schooling Workshop* is just one of the audio tape sets available through CLW's catalog/magazine *Our Family's Favorites*. Various instructional videos are also available through this catalog.

Color the Classics, PO Box 440, Silver Springs NY 14550. *Color the Classics* is a biographical coloring book and cassette tape to help kids learn to love the music and lives of Christ-centered composers. Ages 4-11. $12.95, volumes 1, 2, 3 & 4.

Community Music., Inc., 9428 Curran Road, Silver Spring MD 20901. (301) 434-1181. FAX (301) 445-0939. Award-winning family entertainers Cathy Fink and Marcy Marxer have a new video series: *Song Shop*™. The first two videos in the series, *Is Not, Is Too!* and *Yodel-Ay-Hee-Hoo!* were taped with a family audience in Toronto, Canada, and focus on audience participation. These two entertainers have been together since 1984, and have won such prestigious awards as Parents' Choice Gold Award, Washington Area

Music Association Best Children's Vocalist and Recording. Each video is $14.99.

Davidsons Music, 6726 Metcalf, Shawnee Mission KS 66204. (913) 262-6533. Piano course for Christians. Gives complete foundation in music and emphasizes Christian values and concepts. Preparatory book $7.95. Two cassettes give further explanations, demonstrate music and give advice and encouragement, $10.95 each or $21.90 for both. Book plus both cassettes $27.

Eureka, Lawrence Hall of Science, University of California, Berkeley CA 94720-5200. (510) 642-1016. Educational videos include *Communication*, that teaches children about sound, using four activities, $30.

Facets Multimedia, 1517 West Fullerton Ave., Chicago IL 60614. (312) 281-9075. FAX (312) 929-5437. Toll-free ordering 1-800-331-6197. This company has a special resource called *Facets Non-Violent, Non-Sexist Children's Video Guide,* which is a comprehensive guide to wholesome, entertaining children's videos for children up to 12 years. These films were selected from the

2500 screened, and were chosen not only because they lack sexism or violence, but because of their life-affirming content and cultural diversity. Book is 256 pages, $12.95.

Gateway Films/ Vision Video, 2030 Wentz Church Road, PO Box 540, Worcester PA 19490-0540. (610) 584-1893. FAX (610) 584-4610. Toll-free ordering 1-800-523-0226. This company has a catalog of wonderful videos for children, such as *Charlotte's Web, Pilgrim's Progress, Christy, Anne of Green Gables, The Chronicles of Narnia,* and the *Quigley's Village* series for ages 2-7.

George F. Cram Company, Inc., 301 S. LaSalle St., PO Box 426, Indianapolis IN 46206-0426. (317) 635-5564 FAX (317) 635-2720 Toll-free 1-800-227-4199. This company has been a map publisher since 1867, so it's understandable that they have an unbelievable selection of maps, globes, and atlases.

There's a series of videos for world history: *The Road to Ancient Egypt, The Road to Ancient Greece,* and *The Road to Ancient Rome.* Each program looks at the culture, its rise and fall, its art,

philosophy, architecture, and lifestyle. Each video is $102. This series is also available on CD-ROM.

Other videos available are: *Black History: A Three-Part Series,* $134; *The Declaration of Independence,* $60; *World Geography,* a 6-part series, $208; and *Mythology,* $166. (*Mythology* also available on CD-ROM.) These kinds of materials would be most useful to homeschoolers when purchased as a group so you can split the costs and share the materials.

Great Christian Books, 229 South Bridge Street, PO Box 8000, Elkton MD 21922-8000. (410) 392-0930. Toll-free orders 1-800-775-5422. FAX (410) 392-3103. Internet site: http://www.ssnet.com/~hsguide/online.html Send for special catalog *Homeschool Warehouse.* Satisfaction guaranteed. This is a great one-stop shopping place for homeschooling books of all kinds! There are music education materials, and educational audio-visual materials in this catalog.

Greathall Productions, PO Box 813, Benicia CA 94510. Toll-free 1-800-477-6234. FAX (707) 745-5820. Award-winning storytelling tapes and CDs are produced by this company. These tapes are great family listening and entertainment as well as being a source of enrichment to educational curriculum. Jim Weiss, the narrator, rarely scripts his material before entering the studio, and the result is pure storytelling. Some of the favorites are: *Fairytale Favorites in Story & Song*, winner of 3 awards including Parents' Choice Gold Award; *Greek Myths,* winner of Booklist Annual Editor's Choice; *Arabian Nights,* winner of Parents' Choice Gold Award; and *The Jungle Book,* winner of Parents' Choice Silver Award. Cassettes are $9.95 each, and CDs (available for all mentioned except *Arabian Nights*) $14.95.

Hear & Learn Publications, 603 SE Morrison Rd., Vancouver WA 98664. (360) 694-0034. Thirteen songs from Laura Ingalls Wilder's lifetime are recorded by musicians specializing in pioneer music. Listeners are invited to listen to rare historical music like *Oft in the Stilly Night*, or more familiar tunes such as *Pop! Goes the Weasel.* The companion book, *Musical Memories of Laura Ingalls Wilder*, features a collection of color pictures and black and white historical pictures. The text by Wilder biographer combines all the Wilder material in an informative package. $19.95 plus $3 shipping.

Holt Associates, 2269 Massachusetts Ave, Cambridge MA 02140. (617) 864-3100. FAX (617) 864-9235. John Holt founded *John Holt's Bookstore,* a catalog through which he sold books about education that he thought were especially good.

Mr. Holt was especially interested in music education for children. In the catalog, there's: *Mrs. Stewart's Piano Lessons*, books 1 and 2, $16 each. There's also a preschool version for $13. For detailed instructions on making your own instruments, there's *Make Mine Music*, $10.95.

Insect Lore, PO Box 1535, Shafter CA 93623. Toll-free 1-800-LIVE BUG. FAX (805) 746-0334. They have a wonderful catalog full of every possible way for children to learn about insects. There are puzzles, kits, displays, games, videos and books.

For videos, there's *"Eyewitness" Bird Video*, which shows birds from their prehistoric beginnings to the present, $12.95; *Bugs Don't Bugs Us,* for preschoolers +, shows kids hopping like grasshoppers, flying like butterflies, and wiggling like worms, $19.95.

Instructional Fair, a division of TS Denison, PO Box 1650, Grand Rapids MI 49501. (616) 363-1290. Toll-free ordering 1-800-443-2976.

They have catalogs of materials for early childhood education and for elementary and middle school.

Classical Music Stories introduces children to the world of classical music, 96 pages, $9.95.

Jordan's Knowledge Nook, 2400 Judson Road, Longview TX 75605. (903) 753-8741. Toll-free 1-800-562-5490. FAX (903) 757-6980. They have a 256-page full-color catalog full of educational materials for reading, math, science, social studies, arts & crafts, music, and more. Since they have so much, I'm going to mention a few unusual products that stood out to me. You'll need to see the whole catalog to get a better idea of what's available.

For music education, they have activity books, awards, charts, manipulatives, cassettes & records, and other supplies. Their *Piggyback®* *Songs Series* of books has new songs sung to the tunes of childhood favorites, $8.95 each. Also available in Spanish, and on cassette ($10.95).

There are daily aerobic activities for children on *Get a Good Start* (cassette, $10.95) and motor skills on *Walk Like the Animals* (cassette $10.95).

We All Live Together (cassette, $10.98, CD $13.98, book $4.98) won a Parent's Choice Award in 1995. It's available in three volumes.

Kimbo Educational, PO Box 477, Long Branch NJ 07740. (908) 229-4949. FAX (908) 870-3340. Toll-free 1-800-631-2187. This company has many interesting activities on tape for kids of many ages, such as: *Joining Hands with Other Lands,* a collection of multicultural songs & games that includes an activity sheet, for ages 5-8; *Insects, Bugs & Squiggly Things* with songs such as "I Love Bugs," "Patty's Pet Python," & "Partners in Nature." Ages 4-9.

Their collection of tapes includes products on: aerobics, dance, phonics, language arts, Native American studies, special education, holidays, science, rhythm band, health, environmental and more. Send for product list.

Kol-Ami, 18 W. 27th St., 10th Floor, New York NY 10001. Customer service (212) 779-7944. FAX (212) 779-7115. Toll-free orders 1-800-393-4AMI. This company has the world's largest selection of Jewish music and videos.

Children's videos from Sesame Street, starring the Sesame Street Muppets with animation and songs are: *The Land of Israel; Kibbutz; The People of Israel; Sing Around the Seasons*, and more.

Lifetime Books & Gifts, 3900 Chalet Suzanne Dr., Lake Wales FL 33853. (941) 676-6311. Toll Free for ordering 1-800-377-0390. From their *The Always Incomplete Resource Guide & Catalog*, ($3) they offer a host of quality educational materials. Educational audio materials are available through the catalog.

Melton Book Company, PO Box 23216, Waco TX 76702-3216. Toll-free ordering 1-800-441-0511. They have a catalog of Christian books and videos for adults and children. Their children's videos include *Noah's Ark,* done with vivid

animation, $12.95; and *The Chronicles of Narnia*, a 3-volume set for $38.95.

Michael Olaf Company, "The Montessori Shop" PO Box 1162, Arcata CA 95521. (707) 826-1557 FAX (707) 826-2243. Catalog of toys and games that are educational and contribute to what the company calls "a prepared environment," conducive to learning. The materials are appropriate for learning within the Montessori method, and available for infants to 12 years. Everything carries a full guarantee. $5.00 for a catalog.

Classical Music Set to Stories is a series which introduces the child to classical music in a way which makes it come alive. Each tape is $7. Some of the stories are: *Once Upon the Thames* (Handel); *Nurse Goose* (set to *Mother Goose Suite)*; Tchaikovsky's *Swan Lake*; *Romeo & Juliet;* and more.

Another excellent idea is the cassette *Teaching Peace Songs,* $9.95.

National Home Education Research Institute, ATTN. Dr. Brian Ray Western Baptist College 5000 Deer Park Dr. SE, Salem OR 97301-9392. (503) 375-7019. Email:

bray@wbc.edu This organization, founded by Dr. Brian Ray, produces quality research on home education, and serves as a clearinghouse of research for home educators, researchers, and policymakers. They have a video, *What Research Says About Home Schooling*, ($24) that describes the facts concerning homeschooling.

New England School Supply, 609 Silver St., PO Box 3004, Agawam MA 01001-8004. (413) 786-9800. FAX toll-free 1-800-272-0101. Customer service toll-free 1-800-628-8608. Parents of young children will love their catalog called *The Book of Early Learning,* with materials for infants, preschool, and kindergarten. There are materials for motor skill development, social development, make-believe, music, arts & crafts, language skills, math, science, social studies, and more.

For music education, there's a *Preschool Rhythm Set* with 6 pieces, $22; a set of *Beginner Rhythm Instruments*, $29.95; and popular Ella Jenkins recordings.

Penton Overseas, Inc., 2470 Impala Drive, Carlsbad CA 92008-7226. (619) 431-0060. Toll-free 1-800-748-5804.

FAX (619) 431-8110. This company specializes in foreign language learning tools. Materials are available for ages 5+, and there are books, audios, videos, CD-ROMs, games and more.

An award-winning program is *Lyric Language®*, which has won a SIVA award, a Benjamin Franklin Award, and more. This series is loved by children, and available on video, audio, and CD-ROM. Languages available: French, German, Italian, Japanese (audio & video only), and Spanish. Audios, $9.95 each, videos $14.95 each, and CD-ROMs $49.95 each.

Habla!® Spanish Video Tutor Program is an award-winning video instruction program that has 2 videos, a 90-minute cassette, and a 350 page manual. Basic Course or Intermediate, $59.95 each.

Redleaf Press, 450 N. Syndicate, Suite 5, St. Paul MN 55104-4125. (612) 641-0305. FAX toll-free 1-800-641-0115. Toll-free 1-800-423-8309. They have a 32-page full-color catalog of materials for parents and children, especially early childhood materials. They carry a video of the popular *Ella Jenkins: For the Family,* a captivating collection of rhythms, instruments, and style, $14.95. For toddlers, there's *Hello, Everybody: Playsongs and Rhymes From a Toddler's World*, ages 1-4, cassette, $9.95.

SRA, Science Research Associates, 70 West Madison, Suite 1400, Chicago IL 60602. (312) 214-7250. They offer reading books on videotape, as well as instructional videos and filmstrips in the areas of science, English, history, and art.

Sycamore Tree, 2179 Meyer Place, Costa Mesa CA 92627. (714) 650-4466 for information about products and services. For ordering, call or FAX toll-free 1-800-779-6750. Internet site: http://www.sycamoretree.com/home.html

In addition to full curriculums, The Sycamore Tree offers individual materials in their comprehensive 112-page catalog. There's a wide selection of over 3,000 items. The catalog is free if you mention this book.

Videos include: *Tales From the Great Book,* Bible stories for children. Cassettes include: *The Bible in Living Sound,* which is the Bible dramatized.

Music education materials include *The Usborne Story of Music* about instruments and musical styles from ancient times to present, and *Learning to Read Music* which is an audio cassette and a booklet to cover the basics.
See ad page 50.

Video Phonics, 220 Church St., St. Martinville LA 70582. Video Phonics is a phonics program that utilizes the convenience of video for effective teaching. The video is 33 minutes of nonstop phonics repetition and contains a table of contents with numbered screens for easy reference. $24.95 plus $3 shipping.

Chapter Sixteen
MULTICULTURAL EDUCATION MATERIALS

This chapter is new to this book. We have added it because teaching about diversity is very important, and should be included in every curriculum. For more resources, there's the *Multicultural Education Resource Guide* by Blue Bird Publishing, order form at the end of this book.

Audio-Forum, 96 Broad St., Guilford CT 06437-2612. (203) 453-9794. FAX (203) 453-9774. Email: 74537.550@Compuserve.com
This company has several catalogs which have audio materials: *The Whole World Language Catalog,* which has foreign language courses; *Guilford Green Tapes,* which has a medley of audio materials, and *About Music,* which contains music education and information about composers.
For children, they have Authentic Indian Legends on audio: *The Little Eagle* (Kiowa); *Creating, Little People, and Rabbit's Short Tail* (Choctaw); and *The Rabbit and the Bear, and Why the Hog's Tail is Flat* (Cherokee); each 30-minute cassette is $11.95.
They also have a series of 25 books *The Peoples of North America: The Immigrant Experience* that shows each culture's immigration, early years in the U.S., and profiles of influential individuals from those groups. Available for: Afro-Americans, Arab-Americans, Jewish-American, Filipino-Americans, Danish-American, Russian-Ameri-

cans, Mexican Americans, and many more, $18.95.

Cobblestone Publishing, Inc., 7 School Road, Peterborough NH 03458-1454. (603) 924-7209. Toll-free 1-800-821-0115. FAX (603) 924-7280. Internet site: http://www.cobblestonepub.com. *Earthmaker's Lodge* is a book that contains Native American folklore, activities, and foods. 160 pages, $17.50.

Contemporary Books,/ Jamestown Publishers, 2 Prudential Plaza, Suite 1200, 180 North Stetson Ave., Chicago IL 60601-6790. Toll-free orders 1-800-621-1918. Toll-free FAX 1-800-998-3103.

One college level reading program (can be used as a high school program) is called: *Selections from the Black* (Books 1 to 4) contain provocative selections by Black writers. The texts are arranged to enhance vocabulary and comprehension skills.

Davidson and Associates, Inc., PO Box 2961, Torrance CA 90509. Customer service toll-free 1-800-545-7677. FAX (310) 793-0603. Internet site: http://www.davd.com. This company has a full-color 48-page catalog of educational

software called *The Educational Advantage*.Many of these products are available in your local software stores.

For early readers(Pre-K to grade 3), there's the multicultural stories of *Magic Tales*™ (each $59.95) with stories that magically come to life: *Baba Yaga and the Magic Geese*™ : *A Russian Folk Tale; Imo and the King*™ : *An African Folk Tale; The Little Samurai*™ : *A Japanese Folk Tale.*

Drinking Gourd, PO Box 2557, Redmond WA 98073. This is a *Multicultural Home Education Magazine*, published by Donna Nichols-White, started in 1992. The goal of the publication is to explore and celebrate the diversity of homeschool families.

Enslow Publishers, Inc., 44 Fadem Road, Box 699, Springfield NJ 07081-0699. (201) 379-8890. FAX (201) 379-7940. Toll-free ordering 1-800-398-2504. Internet site: http://www.enslow.com

This company has a series *Great African Americans* that has biographies of Mary McLeod Bethune, Satchel Paige, Sojourner Truth, and more, each $11.95. There's also a series *Native American*

Leaders of the Wild West, with biographies of Chief Joseph, Crazy Horse, Geronimo, Sitting Bull, and more, each $13.45.

Free Spirit Publishing, Inc., 400 1st Avenue North Ste. 616, Minneapolis MN 55401. (612) 338-2068. FAX (612) 337-5050. *Respecting Our Differences: A Guide to Getting Along in a Changing World*, for teens, $12.95.

George F. Cram Company, Inc., 301 S. LaSalle St., PO Box 426, Indianapolis IN 46206-0426. (317) 635-5564 FAX (317) 635-2720 Toll-free 1-800-227-4199. This company has been a map publisher since 1867, so it's understandable that they have an unbelievable selection of maps, globes, and atlases. Besides physical and political maps of the U.S. and the world, they have individual state maps, culture and history maps of American Indians, African Americans, Mexican Americans, and Indians of the Southwest.

They have a set of books called Grandfather's Stories. Each book is $6.95 (and whole series is available on CD-ROM for $69.95). There are *Grandfather's Sto-ries from Germany, Grandfather's Stories from Cambodia, Grandfather's Stories from the Philippines, Grandfather's Stories from Viet Nam,* and *Grandfather's Stories from Mexico. Booklist* said that these books are "a useful addition to any collection."

They also have *Your Country Report™ Cultural Kits* for Australia, England, France, Japan, and Switzerland. The kit contains information cards, color photos, money and stamp samples, time/money converter, national anthem, folk music on cassette, souvenir flag. The material is for grades 4-11, and each country is available for $24.95, or all five sets for $99.

Instructional Fair, a division of TS Denison, PO Box 1650, Grand Rapids MI 49501. (616) 363-1290. Toll-free ordering 1-800-443-2976.

They have catalogs of materials for early childhood education and for elementary and middle school.

Multicultural Music teaches kids new songs to familiar melodies about places around the world, preK-4, 160 pages, $14.95. *Famous People Encyclopedia* is a motivating resource the brings the lives of 80 diverse people into the classroom, grades 1-6, 96 pages, $9.95.

Jordan's Knowledge Nook, 2400 Judson Road, Longview TX 75605. (903) 753-8741. Toll-free 1-800-562-5490. FAX (903) 757-6980. They have a 256-page full-color catalog full of educational materials for reading, math, science, social studies, arts & crafts, music, and more. Since they have so much, I'm going to mention a few unusual products that stood out to me. You'll need to see the whole catalog to get a better idea of what's available.

They have a few multicultural materials, such as *Multi-Ethnic Family Puppets*, $19.95 with a set of 5 (Asian, Hispanic, White, Black).

There's *Multicultural Snacks,* a book with recipes from 38 countries, $6.95.

Multicultural music is also available: *Songs About Native Americans* (ages 4-8, cassette $10.95) includes honor songs; *Multicultural Rhythm Stick Fun* (ages 3-7, cassette $10.95) has rhythm stick activities set to authentic folk tunes & songs from around the world; *Joining Hands With Other Lands* (ages 5-8, cassette $10.95, CD $14.95) helps children learn about people who live in other cultures and countries.

Kimbo Educational, PO Box 477, Long Branch NJ 07740. (908) 229-4949. FAX (908) 870-3340. Toll-free 1-800-631-2187. This company has many interesting activities on tape for kids of many ages, such as: *Joining Hands with Other Lands,* a collection of multicultural songs & more.

Kol-Ami, 18 W. 27th St., 10th Floor, New York NY 10001. Customer service (212) 779-7944. FAX (212) 779-7115. Toll-free orders 1-800-393-4AMI. This company has the world's largest selection of Jewish music and videos.

Children's videos from Sesame Street, starring the Sesame Street Muppets with animation and songs are: *The Land of Israel; Kibbutz; The People of Israel; Sing Around the Seasons,* and more.

Mettanokit, Another Place Conference Center, 173 Merriam Hill Road, Greenville NH 03048. (603) 878-3201. *Return to Creation by Medicine Story,* explains human values and offers solutions to problems confronting people today using the history, traditions and prophecies of his

Wampanoag ancestors, $10. *Children of the Morning Light* by Medicine Story is an illustrated collection of Native American tales and legends of the Wampanoag Nation, $17.

Milliken Publishing Company, 1100 Research Blvd., PO Box 21579, St. Louis MO 63132-0579. (314) 991-4220. Toll-free customer service 1-800-325-4136. Toll-free FAX 1-800-538-1319.

Milliken's catalog of supplementary educational materials contains *Our Global Village* series, which are cultural resource guides, each $6.95. Each guide teaches about the language, holidays, costumes, history, legends, foods, lifestyles, and games of a particular country. Some of the countries in the series are: Australia, Japan, Mexico, Brazil, China, Germany, Russia, Egypt, Poland, Ireland, and Korea.

New England School Supply, 609 Silver St., PO Box 3004, Agawam MA 01001-8004. (413) 786-9800. FAX toll-free 1-800-272-0101. Customer service toll-free 1-800-628-8608. Parents of young children will love their catalog called *The Book of Early Learning,* with materials for in-fants, preschool, and kindergarten. There are materials for motor skill development, social development, make-believe, music, arts & crafts, language skills, math, science, social studies, and more.

They have multicultural materials, such as: *Around the World Soundtracks,* from UNICEF, this game presents authentic sounds from around the world, $14; and *Ethnic Family Puppets*; each family has 4 members, available for Asian family, Black family, Hispanic family, and White family, $28.95 each.

Redleaf Press, 450 N. Syndicate, Suite 5, St. Paul MN 55104-4125. (612) 641-0305. FAX toll-free 1-800-641-0115. Toll-free 1-800-423-8309. They have a 32-page full-color catalog of materials for parents and children, especially early childhood materials. *All The Colors We Are: The Story of How We Get Our Skin Color,* has magnificent photographs and easy-to-understand explanations for children to understand diversity of skin color, ages 4-10, $9.95. They also have a cassette, *A Child's World of Lullabies: Multicultural Songs for Quiet Times,* $9.95.

Chapter Sixteen: Multicultural Education

Scott, Foresman & Company, a subsidiary of HarperCollins Publishers Inc., 1900 E. Lake Ave., Glenview IL 60025. (708) 729-3000. Toll-free 1-800-554-4411. Goodyear Books toll-free 1-800-628-4480, ext. 3038. Major commercial textbook publisher. They have a regular K-8 catalog, and a special catalog for Goodyear Books.

Their Goodyear Books catalog contains a series on *Ancient Living Cultures*, 32 pages each, ages 8+, $9.95 each. The cultures explored are: Eskimos, Celts, China, Egypt, Incas, Great Plains Indians, Rome, Mexico, and more. They also have a book *Notable Women*, that examines the life stories of 23 notable women from around the world, grades 4-6, 128 pages, $9.95.

Skipping Stones Magazine, PO Box 3939, Eugene OR 97403. (541) 342-4956. *Skipping Stones: A Multicultural Children's Magazine,* encourages cooperation, creativity, and environmental awareness. Published bimonthly throughout the school year, it accepts art and original writings in every language and from all ages. Subscription, 5 issues, $20.

Chapter Seventeen

MISCELLANEOUS

Christian Life Workshops (CLW), Box 2250, Gresham OR 97030. (503) 667-3942. Through their catalog/ magazine, *Our Family's Favorites,* they offer some interesting products like educational T-shirts and *The Christian Family's Complete Household Organizer.*

Christian Teaching Materials, PO Box 639, Glenpool OK 74033-0639. (918) 322-3420. Their extensive catalog has products from many different publishers. They have a mailing list of homeschooling families and this list is available for rental. Their *Family Resource Pack* is mailed three times a year to homeschooling families. If you are interested in receiving a copy of the Pack, please let them know you want to be on their mailing list.

Crowder Creations, 451 North 950 East, Orem UT 84057. Toll-free 1-800-273-0372. *How to Sell to the Growing Homeschool Market,* $65.

Follett Home Education, 5563 S. Archer Ave., Chicago IL 60638-3098. Toll-free 1-800-554-5754. They sell used and older textbooks from major publishers. Free catalog.

Home Education and Family Services, PO Box 1056, Gray ME 04039. (207) 657-2800. They provide college admissions assistance.

Home Education Radio Network, PO Box 3338, Idaho Springs CO 80452. (303) 567-4092. Radio show.

Home School Legal Defense Association, PO Box 159,

Paeonian Springs VA 20219. (540) 338-5600. FAX (540) 338-2733. This organization has a syndicated radio show, "Home School Heartbeat," that is a daily two-minute show broadcast on over 150 stations nationwide. You can write for a list of stations at: PO Box 1835, Leesburg VA 20177 or phone (540) 338-5600. This program is designed to encourage home schooling families and to alert the public to the who, what, where, when and why of home schooling.

Homeschool Publishing House/ Homeschool Seller, PO Box 19, Cherry Valley MA 01611-0019, (508) 791-8332. FAX (508) 791-8165. Email: HSSeller@aol.com   This is a home-based business that has a list of used curriculum for sale. Current list $1.75.

Informed Homebirth Informed Birth & Parenting, PO Box 3675, Ann Arbor MI 48106. (313) 662-6857. This organization bases much of their philosophy on Rudolf Steiner, the Austrian educator and founder of the international Waldorf school movement. Many of the books focus on issues on; midwifery, women, homebirth, alternative education, book & video re-

view, and more. Annual membership to this organization is $20.00, included in the membership are 4 issues of their quarterly newsletter, *Special Delivery.*

The Learning Palace, 10134 SE Washington St, Portland OR 97216. (503) 251-1833. Dr. Stewart Wilson is a licensed Educational Psychologist who works with students in many areas: testing, diagnosing learning problems, counseling, and computer assisted tutoring.

Lord's Fine Jewelry, PO Box 486, Piedmont OK 73078-0486. (405) 373-2877. Offers a class ring for home homeschoolers. Available in 10 Kt, 14 Kt yellow or white gold or sterling silver. Send for catalog ($1).

Paradigm Company, Box 45161, Boise ID 83711. (208) 322-4440. There are classic books by Samuel L. Blumenfeld that I recommend be read by parents interested in homeschooling: *NEA, Trojan Horse in American Education,* $14.95; *Is Public Education Necessary?* $19.95. These books were very influential in forming my opinions about public education and the need for homeschooling. There's a new book available called *Whole Language—OBE Fraud,* which explains how the whole concept of whole language for teaching reading was not only misguided, but virtually a fraud, $19.95.

Parents' Rights, 12571 Northwinds Drive, St. Louis MO 63146. (314) 434-4171.

Parents' Rights, a quarterly newsletter is just one of the publication this active group publishes. This group also participates in legal action, hosts educational conferences, provides speakers for conferences and meetings, supports private school, and is active in many other activities as well. A yearly subscription is $15.00 (prices include postage).

Directory

Abbott Computer Training, Inc., PO Box 77527, Steamboat Springs CO 80477. (970) 870-6673. 60,75

A Beka Book®, PO Box 18000, Pensacola FL 32523-9160. Toll-free 1-800-874-2352. 14, 24

Academic Therapy Publications, Ann Arbor Publishers High Noon Books, 20 Commercial Blvd., Novato CA 94949. (415) 883-3314. Toll-free 1-800-422-7249. FAX (415) 883-3720. 14

Alaska Private & Home Education Association (APHEA), PO Box 141764, Anchorage AK 99514. (907) 696-0641. 121, 131

Alexander Graham Bell Association for the Deaf Inc., 3417 Volta Place NW, Washington D.C. 20007-2778. 108

Alliance for Parental Involvement in Education, Inc., PO Box 59, East Chatham NY 12060-0059. (518) 392-6900. Email: allpie@taconic.net Internet site: http://www.croton.com/allpie/

Alpha Omega Publications, 300 N. McKemy Ave, Chandler AZ 85226-2618. (602) 438-2717 Toll-free 1-800-622-3070 FAX (602) 940-8924. Email: aop@home-schooling.com Internet site: http:www.home-schooling.com 14, 25, 60, 85, 99, 141

Alta Vista Curriculum, 12324 Rd 37, Madera CA 93638. (209) 645-4083. Toll-free 1-800-544-1397. 14, 86

American Foundation for the Blind, 11 Penn Plaza, Suite 300, New York NY 10001-2018. (212) 620-2000. TDD (212) 620-2158. 109

American Montessori Consulting, 11961 Wallingsford Rd, PO Box 5062, Rossmoor CA 90720. (310) 598-2321. Email: amonco@aol.com Internet site: http://members.aol.com/amonco/amonco.html 99

American Science and Surplus, 3605 Howard Avenue, Skokie IL 60076. (847) 982-0870. FAX toll-free 1-800-934-0722. 15

American Speech-Language-Hearing Association, 10801 Rockville Pike, Rockville MD 20852. Toll free voice/TDD 1-800-638-8255. 109

Ampersand Press, 750 Lake St., Port Townsend WA 98368. (360) 379-5187. Toll-free 1-800-624-4263. FAX (360) 379-0324. 53

Animal Town, PO Box 485, Healdsburg CA 95448. Toll-free customer service 1-800-445-8642. FAX (707) 837-9737. 53

Aristoplay, Ltd., PO Box 7028, Ann Arbor MI 48107. (313) 995-4353. FAX (313) 995-4611. Toll-free customer service 1-800-634-7738. 54

Arizona Families for Home Education, PO Box 4661, Scottsdale AZ 85161-4661. (602) 443-0612. 121

Arkansas Christian Home Education Association, Box 4410, North Little Rock AR 72116. (501) 758-9099. 122

ArsNova, Box 637, Kirkland WA 98083-0637. (206) 828-2711. FAX (206) 889-0359. Toll-free 1-800-445-4866. 61

At Our Own Pace, 102 Willow Drive., Waukegan IL 60087. 109

Atrium Society Publications, PO Box 816, Middlebury VT 05753. Toll Free 1-800-848-6021. 76

Audio-Forum, 96 Broad St., Guilford

CT 06437-2612. (203) 453-9794. FAX (203)453-9774. Email:74537.550 @Compuserve.com 141, 151

Autism Research Institute, 4182 Adams Avenue, San Diego CA 92116. 110

Backyard Scientist, PO Box 16966, Irvine CA 92713 (714) 551-2392. Email: Backyrdsci@aol.com 25

B.E.A.C.H., 1305 White Marlin Lane, Virginia Beach VA 23464. (804) 474-0389. FAX (804) 579-6114. Email: dplast@exis.net Internet site: http://wwwp.exis.net/~dplast/beach.htm 129, 131

Bend Cornerstone Books, 62570 Dixon Loop, Bend OR 97701. Toll-free 1-800-487-5952. 26, 142

Bea's Penmanship and Creative Writing Program, PO Box 50284, Billings MT 59105. (406) 259-3050. Email: beas@men.net Internet site: http://dns.mcn.net:80/~beas/ 26

Bible Study Guide for All Ages, PO Box 2608, Russellville AR 72811. 86

Blue Bird Publishing, 2266 S. Dobson, Suite #275, Mesa AZ 85202. (602) 831-6063. FAX (602) 831-1829. Email: bluebird@bluebird1.com Web Site: http://www.bluebird1.com 10, 26, 100, 116, 138

Bluestocking Press, PO Box 2030, Shingle Springs CA 95682-2030. (916) 621-1123. Toll-free 1-800-959-8586. FAX (916) 642-9222. 26, 27, 76, 116

Bob Jones University Press, Greenville SC 29614-0001. Toll-free 1-800-845-5731. FAX toll-free 1-800-524-8398. Free home school brochure, call 1-800-739-8199. 15, 61, 77, 86, 100, 142

Boiling Area Home Schoolers of D.C., 1516 E Carswell Circle, Washington DC 20036. 123

Bolchazy-Carducci Publishers, 1000 Brown St., Unit 101, Wauconda IL 60084. (847) 526-4344. FAX (847) 526-2867. 28, 61

Boodle: By Kids for Kids, PO Box 1049, Portland IN 47371. 77

Bornstein School of Memory Training, 11693 San Vicente Blvd., Los Angeles CA 90049. (310) 478-2056. Credit card orders toll-free 1-800-468-2058. 28, 142

Boy Scouts of America, Magazine Division, 1325 Walnut Hill Lane, Irving TX 75083-3096. (214) 580-2000. 77

Bradshaw Publishers, PO Box 277, Bryn Mawr CA 92318. (909) 796-6766. 77, 86

Bread Ministries Inc., PO Box 1017, Arcadia FL 33821-1017. 87

Brigham Young University, Independent Study, 206 Harman Building, PO Box 21514, Provo UT 84602-1514. (801) 378-2868. Toll-free 1-800-298-8792. 15

Broderbund Software, PO Box 6144, Novato CA 94948-6144. (415) 382-4400. 62

Brook Farms Books, PO Box 246, Bridgewater ME 04735. 101

Builder Books, PO Box 99, Riverside WA 98849. (509) 826-6021. Toll-free orders 1-800-260-5461. 54, 87, 143

California Home Educators, 10489 Sunland Blvd., PO Box 4070, Sunland CA 91040. (818) 951-9652. Toll-free 1-800-525-4419. FAX (818) 951-5963. Email: aq483@lafn.org 122

Calvert School, 105 Tuscany Road, Baltimore MD 21210. (410) 243-6030. 15

Carolina Biological Supply Company, 2700 York Road., Burlington NC 27215-3398. (910) 584-0381. Toll-free 1-800-

334-5551. Toll-free FAX 1-800-222-7112. Internet site: http//www.carosci.com 29, 54, 62, 143

Catholic Home School Newsletter, 688 11th Ave NW, New Brighton MN 55112. (612) 636-5761. 132

Caxton Printers, Ltd., 312 Main St., Caldwell ID 83605-3299. (208) 459-7421. FAX (208) 459-7450. Toll-free 1-800-657-6465. 77

Center for Self Sufficiency, PO Box 416, Denver CO 80201-0416. (303) 575-5676. 117

Children's Art Foundation, PO Box 83, Santa Cruz CA 95063. Toll-free 1-800-447-4569. 77

Children's Better Health Institute, 1100 Waterway Blvd., PO Box 567, Indianapolis IN 46206. (317) 636-8881. 78

Children's Bible Hour, Box 1, Grand Rapids MI 49501. Internet site: http://www.gospelcom.net/cbh/ 87

Children's Books at Discount Prices, PO Box 19069, Denver CO 80219. (303) 237-4989. 78

Children's Small Press Collection, 719 N. Fourth Ave., Ann Arbor MI 48104. (313) 668-8056. Toll-free 1-800-221-8056. 29, 78, 95, 110, 117, 143

Children's Television Workshop, 1 Lincoln Plaza, New York NY 10023. (212) 595-3456. 79

Christian Family Resources, PO Box 213, Kit Carson CO 80825-0213. (719) 962-3228. 30

Christian Home Education Association of Austin, PO Box 141998, Austin TX 78714-1998. (512) 450-0070. 128, 132

Christian Home Education Association of West Virginia, PO Box 8770, South Charleston WV 25303. (304) 776-4664. 130

Christian Home Education Confederation of Kansas, PO Box 3564, Shawnee Mission KS 66203. (316) 945-0810. 124

Christian Home Education Fellowship of Alabama, PO Box 563, Alabaster AL 35007. (205) 664-2232. 121

Christian Home Education Support Services of Oregon, PO Box 13693, Portland OR 97213-0693. (503) 784-4398. 127

Christian Home Educator's Association, PO Box 2009, Norwalk CA 90651-2009. (310) 864-3747. 122, 132, 138

Christian Home Educators Coalition, Box 470322, Chicago IL 60647. (312) 278-0673. 123

Christian Home Educators Network, 304 N. Beechwood Ave., Catonsville MD 21228. (410) 744-8919. (410) 444-5465. 125

Christian Home Educators of Arizona (CHEA), PO Box 13445, Scottsdale AZ 85267-3445. 122

Christian Home Educators of Colorado, 1015 S. Gaylord St #226, Denver CO 80209. (303) 388-1888. (303) 777-1022. 122, 132, 138

Christian Home Educators of Kentucky (CHEK), 691 Howardstown Road, Hodgenville KY 42748. (502) 358-9270. 124

Christian Home Educators of New Hampshire, PO Box 961, Manchester NH 03105. 126

Christian Home Educators of Ohio, PO Box 262, Columbus OH 43216. (614) 474-3177. 127

Christian Home Educators of Vermont, 2 Webster St., Barre VT 05641.

(802) 476-8821. 129

Christian Home Educators Fellowship of Louisiana (CHEF), PO Box 74292, Baton Rouge LA 70784-4292. (504) 775-9709. 124

Christian Home Educators Fellowship of Oklahoma, PO Box 471363, Tulsa OK 74147-1363. (918) 583-7323. 127

Christian Home School Association of Pennsylvania, PO Box 3603, York PA 17402-0603. (717) 661-2428. 127

Christian Homeschoolers of Hawaii, 91-824 Oama St, Ewa Beach HI 96706. (808) 689-6398. 123

Christian Liberty Academy Satellite Schools, 502 W. Euclid Ave, Arlington Heights IL 60004. (847) 259-4444. FAX (847) 259-2941. 16, 87

Christian Life Workshops (CLW), Box 2250, Gresham OR 97030. (503) 667-3942. 10, 16, 30, 55, 87, 96, 101, 117, 120, 132, 144, 157

Christian Schools International, 3350 East Paris Ave SE, Grand Rapids MI 49512-3054. Toll-free 1-800-635-8288. 16

Christian Teaching Materials, PO Box 639, Glenpool OK 74033-0639. (918) 322-3420. 157

Clonlara School, 1289 Jewett, Ann Arbor MI 48104. (313) 769-4515. Email: clonlara@delphi.com Internet site: http://web.grfn.org/education/clonlara 16, 63

Cobblestone Publishing, Inc., 7 School Road, Peterborough NH 03458-1454. (603) 924-7209. Toll-free 1-800-821-0115. FAX (603) 924-7280. Internet site: http://www.cobblestonepub.com. 79, 152

Color the Classics, PO Box 440, Silver Springs NY 14550. 87, 144

Common Sense Press, PO Box 5863, Hollywood FL 33083. (305) 962-1930. FAX (305) 964-7644. 17, 96, 101

Community Music., Inc., 9428 Curran Road, Silver Spring MD 20901. (301) 434-1181. FAX (301) 445-0939. 144

Concord Review: A Quarterly Review of Essays by Students of History, PO Box 661, Concord MA 01742. (508) 331-5007. Email: fitzhugh@tcr.org 79, 81

Consumers Unions of U.S., Inc., PO Box 57777, Yonkers NY 10703. (914) 378-2000. 80

Contemporary Books,/ Jamestown Publishers, 2 Prudential Plaza, Suite 1200, 180 North Stetson Ave., Chicago IL 60601-6790. Toll-free orders 1-800-621-1918. Toll-free FAX 1-800-998-3103. 30

Council for Exceptional Children, 1920 Association Drive, Reston VA 22091-1589. Toll-free 1-800-CEC-READ (232-7323). TTY: (703) 264-9446. FAX (703) 264-1637. Email: cecpubs@cec.sped.org 110

Creation's Child, PO Box 3004 #44, Corvallis OR 97339. (541) 758-3413. 31, 87

Creative Home Teaching, PO Box 152581, San Diego CA 92105. (619) 263-8633. 31, 88, 96

Cricket Magazine Group, PO Box 7434, Red Oak IA 51591-4434. Order toll-free 1-800-827-0227. 80

Critical Thinking Books & Software, PO Box 448, Pacific Grove CA 93950-0448. (408) 393-3288. FAX (408) 393-3277. Toll-free 1-800-458-4849. Email: ctpress@aol.com. 63

Crossings®, 6550 E. 30th St., PO Box 6325, Indianapolis IN 46206-6325. (317) 541-8920. 88

Crowder Creations, 451 North 950 East, Orem UT 84057. Toll-free 1-800-273-0372. 157

Cuisenaire Company, 10 Bank St., PO Box 5026, White Plains NY 10602-5026. Customer service toll-free 1-800-237-3142. Orders toll-free 1-800-237-0338. FAX toll-free 1-800-551-RODS. Internet site: http://www.cuisenaire.com. 31, 64, 111

Cygnet Press, Inc., HC 12, Box 7A, 116 Hwy 28, Anthony NM 88021. (505) 874-3306. 32, 101

Cystic Fibrosis Foundation, 6931 Arlington Road, Bethesda MD 20814. (301) 951-4422. 1-800-FIGHT CF. 111

Davda Corporation, 7074 N. Western Ave., Chicago IL 60645. (312) 465-4070 FAX (312) 262-9298 Internet site: http://www.davka.com 64

Davidson and Associates, Inc., PO Box 2961, Torrance CA 90509. Customer service toll-free 1-800-545-7677. FAX (310) 793-0603. Internet site: http://www.davd.com. 64, 152

Davidsons Music, 6726 Metcalf, Shawnee Mission KS 66204. (913) 262-6533. 144

Delaware Home Education Association, 11 Bristol Knoll Rd., Newark, DE 19711. (302) 633-8528 FAX (302) 993-5950. 123, 132

Design-a-Study, 408 Victoria Avenue, Wilmington DE 19804-2124. (302) 998-3889. 32

Discovery Toys, Inc., 6400 Brisa St., Livermore CA 94550. (510) 606-2600. FAX (510) 447-0626. Toll-free 1-800-426-4777. 55, 117

Division of Independent Study, 1510 12th Ave. N., PO Box 5036, State University Station, Fargo ND 58105-5036. (701) 231-6000. Internet site: http://www.uol.com/ndak 17

Doorposts, Suite 372, PO Box 1610, Clackamas OR 97015. (503) 698-7973. 88

The Doula, PO Box 71, Santa Cruz CA 95063-0071. Phone/FAX (408) 464-9488. Toll-free orders 1-800-MY-DOULA. 117

Drinking Gourd, PO Box 2557, Redmond WA 98073. 32, 132, 152

ESP Publishers, Inc., 7163 123rd Circle N., Largo FL 34643. Toll-free 1-800-643-0280. 32

Edmark, 6727 185th Ave NE, PO Box 97021, Redmond WA 98073-9721. (206) 556-8400. FAX (206) 556-8430. Toll-free ordering 1-800-362-2890. Customer Service Email: edmarkteam@edmark.com Internet site: http://www.edmark.com 65

Education Association of Christian Homeschoolers, 25 Fieldstone Run, Farmington CT 06032. 123

Education Network of Christian Homeschoolers, 120 Mayfair Lane, Mount Laurel NJ 08054. (609) 222-4823. 126

Education Services, 8825 Blue Mountain Drive, Golden CO 80403. 1-800-421-6645. 102

The Elijah Company, Route 2, Box 100-B, Crossville TN 38555. (615) 456-6284. FAX (615) 456-6384. 33, 96

Engine-Uity, Ltd., PO Box 9610, Phoenix AX 85068. (602) 997-7144. FAX (602) 995-0974. Toll-free ordering 1-800-877-8718. 33

Enslow Publishers, Inc., 44 Fadem Road, Box 699, Springfield NJ 07081-0699. (201) 379-8890. FAX (201) 379-7940. Toll-free ordering 1-800-398-2504. Internet site: http://www.enslow.com 80, 152

Essential Learning Products Company, 2300 West Fifth Ave., PO Box 2607, Columbus OH 43216-2607 (614) 486-0631. FAX (614) 487-2700. 33, 55

Eureka, Lawrence Hall of Science, University of California, Berkeley CA 94720-5200. (510) 642-1016. 34, 144

Facets Multimedia, 1517 West Fullerton Ave., Chicago IL 60614. (312) 281-9075. FAX (312) 929-5437. Toll-free ordering 1-800-331-6197. 144

Families for Home Education, 400 E. High Point Lane, Columbia MO 65203. (816) 826-9302. 126

Families Honoring Christ, Earl & Diane Rodd, 2180 Northland Ave, Lakewood OH 44107. 89

Family Educators Alliance of South Texas, 4719 Blanco Rd., San Antonio TX 78212. (210) 342-4674. 128

The Family Store, 330 McEnery Road., Felton CA 95018. 118

FergNus Services, PO Box 578, Richlandtown PA 18955-0578. (610) 282-0401. FAX (610) 282-0402. 102

Flagstaff Home Educators, 6910 West Suzette Lane, Flagstaff AZ 86001-8220. (520) 774-0806. 122

Florida Parent-Educators Association, 3781 SW 18th St., Ft. Lauderdale FL 33312. (407) 723-1714. 123

Follett Home Education, 5563 S. Archer Ave., Chicago IL 60638-3098. Toll-free 1-800-554-5754. 157

Fort Wayne Area Home Schools, PO Box 12954, Fort Wayne IN 46866-2954. (219) 483-2807. 124

Free Spirit Publishing, Inc., 400 1st Avenue North Ste. 616, Minneapolis MN 55401. (612) 338-2068. FAX (612) 337-5050. 82, 111, 153

Front Row Experience, 540 Discovery Bay Blvd., Byron CA 94514-9454. (510) 634-5710. 34, 112

Gateway Films/ Vision Video, 2030 Wentz Church Road, PO Box 540, Worcester PA 19490-0540. (610) 584-1893. FAX (610) 584-4610. Toll-free ordering 1-800-523-0226. 89, 145

Gazelle Publications, 9853 Jericho Road, Bridgman MI 49106-9742. (616) 465-4004. Toll-free 1-800-650-5076. Email: wadeted@aol.com 10, 102

George F. Cram Company, Inc., 301 S. LaSalle St., PO Box 426, Indianapolis IN 46206-0426. (317) 635-5564 FAX (317) 635-2720 Toll-free 1-800-227-4199. 34, 36, 66, 145, 153

Georgia Home Education Association, 245 Buckeye Lane, Fayetteville GA 30214. (404) 461-3657. 123

God's World Publications Inc., 85 Tunnel Rd. Innsbruck Mall, PO Box 2330, Asheville NC 28802-2330. Toll Free 1-800-951-5437. 89

Good News Publishers, Crossway Books, 1300 Crescent St., Wheaton IL 60187. FAX (708) 682-4785. Toll-free ordering 1-800-323-3890. 89, 102

Great Christian Books, 229 South Bridge Street, PO Box 8000, Elkton MD 21922-8000. (410) 392-0930. Toll-free orders 1-800-775-5422. FAX (410) 392-3103. Email: gcb@ssnet.com Internet site: http:www.GreatChristianBooks.com 17, 35, 55, 66, 82, 90, 103, 118, 145

Greathall Productions, PO Box 813, Benicia CA 94510. Toll-free 1-800-477-6234. FAX (707) 745-5820. 145

Great Lakes Christian Educators' Convention, 8585 Dixie Hwy, Clarkston MI 48348. (810) 625-2311. 125

Greenhaven Press, Inc., PO Box 289009, San Diego CA 92198-9009. FAX (619) 485-9549. Toll-free ordering 1-800-231-5163. 35

Green Pastures Press, 7102 Lynn Road NE, Minerva OH 44657. (33) 895-3291. 90

HCL, PO Box 4643, Whittier CA 90607. (310) 696-4696. 120

HEC Reading Horizons, 3471 South 550 West, Bountiful UT 84010. Toll-free 1-800-333-0059. 35, 67

Hands-On Equations, Borenson and Associates, PO Box 3328, Allentown PA 18106. Toll-free 1-800-993-6284. 37, 55

Hands On History, 201 Constance Drive, New Lenox IL 60451. 37

HarperCollins Publishers, Inc., School Division, 10 E. 53rd St., New York NY 10022-5299. Toll-free 1-800-331-3761. 27

Hear & Learn Publications, 603 SE Morrison Rd., Vancouver WA 98664. (360) 694-0034. 146

Hearthsong, 170 Professional Center Drive, Rohnert Park CA 94928-2149. Toll-free 1-800-325-2502. 56

Hewitt Homeschooling Resources, PO Box 9, Washougal WA 98671-0009. (360) 835-8708. FAX (360) 835-8697. 17, 37, 90, 103, 112

Highlights for Children (and Essential Learning Products Company), PO Box 269, 2300 W. 5th Ave., Columbus OH 43272-0002. (614) 486-0695. FAX (614) 487-2700. Toll-free 1-800-255-9517. 82

Holt Associates, 2269 Massachusetts Ave, Cambridge MA 02140. (617) 864-3100. FAX (617) 864-9235. 17, 36, 37, 56, 103, 120, 132, 146

Holt, Rinehart & Winston, School Division, 1627 Woodland Ave., Austin TX 78741. Orders call toll-free to California office 1-800-222-4658. 38

Home Education Action Council of Ohio, PO Box 24133, Huber Heights OH 45424. (513) 242-9226. 127

Home Education and Family Services, PO Box 1056, Gray ME 04039. (207) 657-2800. 104, 133, 134

Home Education Press, PO Box 1083, Tonasket WA 98855. (509) 486-1351. FAX (509) 486-2628. Toll-free ordering 1-800-236-3278.Email: HomeEdMag @aol.com Internet site: http://www. home-edpress.com 127

Home Education Radio Network, PO Box 3338, Idaho Springs CO 80452. (303) 567-4092. 157

Home Educators Association of Virginia, 1900 Byrd Avenue, Suite 201, PO Box 6745, Richmond VA 23230. (804) 288-1608. FAX (804) 288-6962. 129, 133

Homefires, 180 El Camino Real, Suite 10, Millbrae CA 94030. (415) 365-9425. 133

Home Life, PO Box 1250, 1731 Smizer Mill Rd., Fenton MO 63026-1850. (314) 225-9790. FAX (314) 225-0743. 133

Home-Oriented Private Education for Texas, PO Box 59876, Dallas TX 75229-9876. (214) 358-2221. 128

Home Run Enterprises, 16172 Huxley Circle, Westminister CA 92683. (714) 841-1220. FAX (714) 841-5584. Email: Caduffy@aol.com 104

Home School Association of California, PO Box 2442, Atascadero CA 93423. 122

Home School Books & Supplies, 104 S. West Ave., Arlington WA 98223. (360) 435-0376. FAX (360) 435-1028. Toll-free orders 1-800-788-1221. Internet site: http://www.thehomeschool.com 38

Homeschoolers of Maine, HC 62 Box 24, Hope ME 04847. (207) 763-4251. 124, 133, 138

Homeschoolers of Wyoming, 339 Bicentennial Court, Powell WY 82435. (307) 754-3271. 133

Homeschooling Clearinghouse, PO Box 293023, Sacramento CA 95829-3023. (916) 422-2879. Email: hicnews@aol.com 120

Homeschooling Today, PO Box 9596, Birmingham AL 35220. 134

Home School Legal Defense Association, PO Box 159, Paeonian Springs VA 20219. (540) 338-5600. FAX (540) 338-2733. 10, 138, 157

Homeschool Marketing Group, Inc., 6226 NE 182nd St., Seattle WA 98155. Toll-free ordering 1-800-481-3466. 38

Homeschool Publishing House/ Homeschool Seller, PO Box 19, Cherry Valley MA 01611-0019, (508) 791-8332. FAX (508) 791-8165. Email: HSSeller@aol.com 104, 158

Home School Supply House, PO Box 2000, Beaver UT 84713. (801) 438-1254. 38

Home Schools United—Vegas Valley, PO Box 93564, Las Vegas NY 89193. (702) 870-9566. 126, 134

Home School Support Network of Michigan, PO Box 2457, Riverview MI 48192. (313) 284-1249. 125, 135

Home Study International, 12501 Old Columbia Pike, Silver Spring MD 20904-6600. (301) 680-6570. FAX (301) 680-6577. Toll-free 1-800-782-GROW (4769). 18

Home Teachers, PO Box 8724, Stockton CA 95208-0724. 38

Howshall Home Publications, 9508 203rd Ave. E, Sumner WA 98390. 90

ICER Press Bookstore, PO Box 877, Claremount CA 91711. 105

Idaho Home Educators, PO Box 1324, Meridian ID 83680-1324. (208) 482-7336. 123, 135

Illinois Christian Home Educators, PO Box 261, Zion Ill 60099. (708) 662-0230. 118, 124

Incentive Publications, 3835 Cleghorn Ave., Nashville TN 37215-2532. (615) 385-2934. FAX (615) 385-2967. Toll-free 1-800-421-2830. 38, 112

Indiana Association of Home Educators, 1000 N. Madison, Suite S2, Greenwood IN 46142. (317) 770-0644. 124

Information Network for Christian Homes, 4934 Cannonsburg Road, Belmont MI 49306. (616) 874-5656. 125

In One EAR Publications, 29481 Manzanita Drive, Campo CA 91906-1128. 39

Informed Homebirth Informed Birth & Parenting, PO Box 3675, Ann Arbor MI 48106. (313) 662-6857. 139, 158

Inland Empire Home School Center, PO Box 1750, Airway Heights WA 99001. Toll-free 1-800-378-4699. 18, 129, 135

Insect Lore, PO Box 1535, Shafter CA 93623. Toll-free 1-800-LIVE BUG. FAX (805) 746-0334. 39, 146

Instructional Fair, PO Box 1650, Grand Rapids MI 49501. (616) 363-1290. Toll-free ordering 1-800-443-2976. 39, 147, 153

International Linguistics Corp., 3505 E. Red Bridge Road, Kansas City MO 64137. (816) 765-8855. Toll-free 1-800-237-1830. 18

Jordan's Knowledge Nook, 2400 Judson Road, Longview TX 75605. (903) 753-8741. Toll-free 1-800-562-5490. FAX (903) 757-6980. 40, 56, 147, 154

Kentucky Home Education Association, PO Box 81, Winchester KY 40392-0081. (606) 744-8562. 124

KidsArt, PO Box 274, Mt. Shasta CA 96067. Phone and FAX (916) 926-5076. Email: kidsart@macshasta.com Internet site: http://www.merrymac.com/mspage/kidsart/kahome.html 41

Kimbo Educational, PO Box 477, Long Branch NJ 07740. (908) 229-4949. FAX (908) 870-3340. Toll-free 1-800-631-2187. 147, 154

Kol-Ami, 18 W. 27th St., 10th Floor, New York NY 10001. Customer service (212) 779-7944. FAX (212) 779-7115. Toll-free orders 1-800-393-4AMI. 148, 154

Konos Curriculum, PO Box 1534, Richardson TX 75083. (214) 669-8337. 91, 96, 139

Landmark Distributors, PO Box 849, Fillmore CA 93015. (805) 524-3263. 18, 91

Landmark's Freedom Baptist Curriculum, 2222 E. Hinson Ave., Hinson City FL 33844-4902. FAX (941) 422-0188. Toll-free 1-800-700-LFBC. 91, 139

Leadership Resources, PO Box 413, New Lenox IL 60451. (815) 485-4900. FAX (815) 485-4995. Toll-free ordering 1-800-572-6657. 91

Learn Inc., 113 Gaither Drive, Mt. Laurel NJ 08054. Toll-free 1-800-729-7323. FAX (609) 273-7766. 41

Learning Company, 6493 Kaiser Drive, Fremont CA 94555. Toll-free 1-800-852-2255. 67

Learning disAbilities Resources, PO Box 716, Bryn Mawr, PA 19010. (610) 525-8336. Toll Free 1-800-869-8336. 112

The Learning Edge, 4813 E. Marshall Dr., Vestal NY 13850. (607) 722-6563. 57

The Learning Palace, 10134 SE Washington St, Portland OR 97216. (503) 251-1833. 158

Leonardo Press, PO Box 1326, Camden ME 04843. 19, 41

Lifetime Books & Gifts, 3900 Chalet Suzanne Dr., Lake Wales FL 33853. (941) 676-6311. Toll Free for ordering 1-800-377-0390. 42, 58, 83, 91, 97, 105, 113, 148

Li'l Journeys Educational Products, 4600 Morningstar Drive. PO Box 26565, Prescott Valley AZ 86312. Toll-free 1-800-442-7432. 41, 57

Lord's Fine Jewelry, PO Box 486, Piedmont OK 73078-0486. (405) 373-2877. 158

Loving Education at Home, PO Box 88, Cato NY 13003. (716) 346-0939. 126

Luvmour Family, PO Box 445, N. San Juan CA 95960. (916) 292-3858. Email: pathfinder@oro.net Internet site: http://www.oro.net/~pathfinder/pf.htm 97

M&M Software, PO Box 15769, Long Beach CA 90815. (310) 420-2655. FAX (310) 420-2955. Toll-free 1-800-642-6163. Email: mmsoft@aol.com 68

MacSoft, The WizardWorks Group, 3850 Annapolis Lane, Ste 100, Minneapolis MN 55447-5443. (612) 559-5301. Toll-free 1-800-229-2714. FAX (612) 577-0631. 68

March of Dimes, Birth Defects Foundation, National Headquarters, 1275 Mamaroneck Ave., White Plains NY 10605. (914) 428-7100. Toll-free 1-800-367-6630. 113

Maryland Association of Christian Home Education Organizations, PO Box 3964, Frederick MD 21705. (301) 663-3999. 125

Massachusetts Homeschool Organization of Parent Educators, 15 Ohio St., Wilmington MA 01887. (508) 658-8970. 125, 135

Math Teachers Press, 5100 Gamble Drive, Suite 398, Minneapolis MN 55416. (612) 545-6535. Toll-free 1-800-852-6535. 42

Maupin House Publishing, PO Box 90148 32 SW 42 Street, Gainesville Fl 32607. Phone or FAX (904) 373-5588. Toll-free 1-800-524-0634. 42

McGuffey Academy International, PO Box 109, Lakemont GA 30552. (706) 782-7709. 19, 42

Melton Book Company, PO Box 23216, Waco TX 76702-3216. Toll-free ordering 1-800-441-0511. 91, 148

Meridian Creative Group, 5178 Station Road, Erie PA 16510-4636. (814) 898-2612. Toll-free 1-800-695-9427. FAX (814) 898-0683. Internet site: www.meridiancg.com 69

Merlyn's Pen, PO Box 1058, Greenwich RI 02818. Toll-free 1-800-247-2027. 83

Mettanokit, Another Place Conference Center, 173 Merriam Hill Road, Greenville NH 03048. (603) 878-3201. 154

Michael Olaf Company, "The Montessori Shop" PO Box 1162, Arcata CA 95521. (707) 826-1557 FAX (707) 826-2243. 42, 58, 148

Milliken Publishing Company, 1100 Research Blvd., PO Box 21579, St. Louis MO 63132-0579. (314) 991-4220. Toll-free customer service 1-800-325-4136. Toll-free FAX 1-800-538-1319. 42, 69, 155

Mindscape, 88 Rowland Way, Novato CA 94945. Toll-free ordering 1-800-231-3088. FAX (415) 897-9956. 90

Minnesota Association of Christian Home Educators, (MACHE), PO Box 32308, Fridley MN 55432-0308. (612) 717-9070. 125

Mississippi Home Educators Association, Route 9, Box 350, Laurel MS 39440. (601) 649-MHEA. 125

Missouri Association of Christian Teaching Homes, 307 E. Ash St., #146, Columbia MO 65201. (314) 443-8217. 126

Montana Coalition of Home Schools, PO Box 654, Helena MT 59624. (406) 587-6163. 126

Montessori Services, 836 Cleveland Ave., Santa Rosa, CA 95401 (707) 579-3003. FAX (707) 579-1604. 43

The Moore Foundation, Box 1, Camas WA 98607. 97, 105, 135, 139

Motes Educational Software, PO Box 575, Siloam Springs AR 72761, (501) 524-8741. Email: 73757.1111 @compuserve.com. Internet site: http:ourworld.compuserve.com/ homepages/schoolmom. 70

Mothers Resource Guide, PO Box 469, Fallston MD 21047. (410) 877-0692. 118, 136

Mountain House Press, Box 353, Philo CA 95466. 105, 139

Mountain Meadow Press, PO Box 318, Sitka AK 99835-0318. Phone/ FAX (907) 747-1026. 106

Muscular Dystrophy Association, 114 Old Country Road, Suite 116, Mineola NY 11501. (718) 793-1100. 113

National Center for Home Education, PO Box 159, Paeonian Springs VA 22129. (703) 338-7600. FAX (703) 338-2733. 121

National Easter Seal Society, 230 West Monroe Street, Suite 1800, Chicago IL 60606. (312) 726-6200. FAX (312) 726-1494. 114

National Federation of the Blind, 1800 Johnson Street, Baltimore MD 21230. (410) 659-9314. 114

National Home Education Research Institute, ATTN. Dr. Brian Ray Western Baptist College 5000 Deer Park Dr. SE, Salem OR 97301-9392. (503) 375-7019. Email: bray@wbc.edu 11, 121, 138, 139, 149, 158

National Teaching Aids Inc., 1845 Highland Ave., New Hyde Park NY 11040. (516) 326-2555. 43

National Wildlife Federation, 1400 16th St., NW, Washington DC 20036-2266. FAX (703) 442-7332. Order toll-free 1-800-432-6564. Customer service toll-free 1-800-822-9919. TDD toll-free 1-800-435-3543. 83

Network of Iowa Christian Home Educators, Box 158, Dexter IA 50070. (515) 789-4310 or toll-free 1-800-723-0438. 124

New Attitude, 6920 SE Hogan, Gresham OR 97080. (503) 669-1236. 136

New England School Supply, 609 Silver St., PO Box 3004, Agawam MA 01001-8004. (413) 786-9800. FAX toll-free 1-800-272-0101. Customer service toll-free 1-800-628-8608. 43, 149, 155

New Mexico Christian Home Educators, 5749 Paradise Blvd., NW, Albuquerque MN 87114. (505) 897-1772. 126

Nordic Software, PO Box 6007, Lincoln NE 68506-0007. (402) 488-5086. FAX (402) 488-2914. Internet site: http://www.nordicsoftware.com/ 70, 75, 92

North Carolinians for Home Education, 419 N. Boylan Ave., Raleigh NC 27603. (919) 834-6243. 126

North Dakota Home School Association, 4007 N. State St., Rt. 5, Box 9, Bismarck ND 58501. (701) 223-4080. 126

Northern Nevada Home Schools, Inc., c/o Connie Packer, 4010 DeSoto Way, Reno NV 89502. 126

Northern Nevada Home Schools, PO Box 21323, Reno NV 89515. (702) 852-6647.

North Georgia Home Education Association, 200 West Crest Road, Rossville GA 30741. 126

North Texas Home Education Network, Box 59627, Dallas TX 75229. (214) 234-2366. 128

Northwest Curriculum Exhibition, 2515 NE 37th Ave., Portland OR 97212. 140

NovaNet Campus™ , University Communications, Inc., 3895 N. Business Center Drive, Suite 120, Tucson AZ 85705. Toll-free 1-800-243-7758. FAX (520) 888-8729. Internet site: http://www.nn.com/campus. Email: campus@nn.com. 71

Oak Meadow School, PO Box 740, Putney VT 05346. (802) 387-2021. 19, 21

Oklahoma Central Home Educators Association, (OCHEC), PO Box 270601, Oklahoma City OK 73137. (405) 521-8439. 127

Oregon Christian Home Education Association (OCEAN), 2515 NE 37th, Portland OR 97212. Phone/FAX (503) 288-1285. 127

Orton Dyslexia Society, Chester Building #382, 8600 LaSalle Road, Baltimore MD 21286. (410) 296-0232. 115

Our Christian Heritage, 7923 West 62nd Way, Arvada CO 80004. (303) 421-0444. 44

Packard Bell Interactive Software, 1201 3rd Ave., #2301, Seattle WA 98101. (206) 654-4100. 71

Parable Publishing, RD 2 Box 2002, Middlebury VT 05753. 106, 140

Paradigm Company, Box 45161, Boise ID 83711. (208) 322-4440. 44, 106, 140, 159

Parenting Press, PO Box 75267, 11065 5th Ave, NE, Suite F, Seattle WA 98125. (206) 364-2900. Toll-free 1-800-99-BOOKS. FAX (206) 364-0802. Internet site: http://www.parentbooks.com/ 97

Parents' Choice, Box 185, Waban, MA 02168. (617) 965-5913. 83

Parents' Rights, 12571 Northwinds Drive, St. Louis MO 63146. (314) 434-4171. 11, 140, 159

Parsons Technology, One Parsons Dr., PO Box 100, Hiawatha IA 52233-0100. (319) 395-9626. Toll-free 1-800-223-6925. FAX (319) 395-7449. 71, 92

Pennsylvania Homeschoolers, RD 2 Box 117, Kittanning PA 16201. (412) 783-6512. 127

Penton Overseas, Inc., 2470 Impala Drive, Carlsbad CA 92008-7226. (619) 431-0060. Toll-free 1-800-748-5804. FAX (619) 431-8110. 44, 72, 149

Peter Marshall Ministries, 81 Finlay Road, Orleans MA 02653. (508) 255-7705. FAX (508) 255-2062. Toll-free 1-800-879-3298. 140

Phoenix Special Programs, 3132 W. Clarendon Ave., Phoenix AZ 85017-4589. (602) 263-5661. 19

Philications, PO Box 6002-17, Virginia Beach VA 23456. (804) 427-0619. 58

Pioneer Productions, PO Box 328, Young AZ 85554. 115

Playfair Toys, PO Box 18210, Boulder CO 80308-8210. Customer Service (303) 440-7229. FAX (303) 440-3393. Toll-free 1-800-824-7255. 44

Portland State University Continuing Education Press, PO Box 1394, Portland OR 97207-1394. (503) 725-4846. 44

Presbyterian Publishing Corporation, 3904 Produce Road, Louisville KY 40218. Toll-free 1-800-227-2872. 92

Providence Project, 14566 NW 110th St., Whitewater KS 67154. (316) 799-2112. 45

Prufrock Press™, PO Box 8813, Waco TX 76714-8813. (817) 756-3337. FAX (817) 756-3339. Toll-free ordering 1-800-998-2208. Toll-free FAX for ordering 1-800-240-0333. Internet site: http://www.purfrock.com 45, 84, 106, 115

Redleaf Press, 450 N. Syndicate, Suite 5, St. Paul MN 55104-4125. (612) 641-0305. FAX toll-free 1-800-641-0115. Toll-free 1-800-423-8309. 45, 97, 149, 155

Rhode Island Guild of Home Teachers, PO Box 11, Hope RI 02831-0011. (401) 821-1546. 127

SRA, Science Research Associates, 70 West Madison, Suite 1400, Chicago IL 60602. (312) 214-7250. 46, 150

S.U.A. Phonics Department, 1339 East McMillan St., Cincinnati, OH 45206. (513) 961-4877. 46, 48

Sacramento Council of Parent Educators (SCOPE), PO Box 163178, Sacramento CA 95816. Phone or FAX (916) 368-0401. 46, 122, 136

Sacramento Surplus Book Room, 4131 Power Inn Rd. Ste. D, Sacramento CA 95826. (916) 454-3459.

Santa Ines Publications, 330 W. Hwy 246 #232, Buellton CA 93427. (805) 688-7862. 48

Saxon Publishers, 1320 West Lindsey St., Norman OK 73069. Toll-free ordering 1-800-284-7019. FAX (405) 360-4205. 20

School Supply Room, 3121 Irishtown Rd., Gordonville PA 17529. 46

School Zone Publishing, 1819 Industrial Drive, PO Box 777, Grand Haven MI 49417. (616) 846-5030. FAX (616) 846-6181. Toll-free 1-800-253-0564. 46, 48, 58, 72

Scott, Foresman & Company, a subsidiary of HarperCollins Publishers Inc., 1900 E. Lake Ave., Glenview IL 60025. (708) 729-3000. Toll-free 1-800-554-4411. Goodyear Books toll-free 1-800-628-4480, ext. 3038. 47, 156

Shady Grove Church, 1829 W. Shady Grove Church, Grand Prairie TX 75050. 20, 92, 136

Shekinah Curriculum Cellar, 101 Meador Road, Kilgore TX 75662. (903) 643-2760. FAX (903) 643-2796. 20, 47

Show Me Math, PO Box 7452, Overland Park KS 66207. (913) 383-5005. 72

Skipping Stones Magazine, PO Box 3939, Eugene OR 97403. (541) 342-4956. 156

Small Ventures, 11023 Watterson Dr., Dallas TX 75228. (214) 681-1728. 47

Socially Redeeming Software, 1717 E. Union Hills #1034, Phoenix AZ 85024. (602) 482-3161. 72

Sound Software, 3905 Coronado, Plano TX 75074. (214) 516-1328. 73

South Carolina Association of Independent Home Schools, PO Box 2104, Irmo SC 29063. (803) 551-1003. 127

South Carolina Home Educators Association, PO Box 612, Lexington SC 29071. (803) 951-8960. 128

Southeast Texas Home School Association, 4950 FM 1960 W., Ste. C3-87, Houston TX 77069. (713) 370-8787. 128

Story Time Stories That Rhyme™, PO Box 416, Denver CO 80201-0416. 49

Straight Edge., Inc., 296 Court St., Brooklyn NY 11231. (718) 643-2794. FAX (718) 403-9582. Toll-free 1-800-READMAT. 49

Summer Island Press, PO Box 279, Williamsburg MI 49690. 106

Summit Christian Academy, DFW Corporate Park, 2100 N. Hwy 360, Suite 503, Grand Prairie TX 75050. Toll-free 1-800-362-9180. 20

Sycamore Tree, 2179 Meyer Place, Costa Mesa CA 92627. (714) 650-4466 for information about products and services. For ordering, call or FAX toll-free 1-800-779-6750. Internet site: http://www.sycamoretree.com/home.html 20, 49, 50, 58, 73, 92, 98, 107, 150

TEACH Services, Donivan Rd., Route 1, Box 182, Brushton NY 12916-9738. (518) 358-2125. Toll-free 1-800-367-1844. FAX (518) 358-3028. 49, 107

Teaching Home, PO Box 20219, Portland OR 97294. (503) 253-9633. Subscription address and phone: PO Box 469069, Escondido CA 92046-9069. Toll-free 1-800-395-7760. 136

Teaching Parents Association, 100 East 109th St. North, Valley Center KS 67147. 124

Tennessee Home Education Association, Smoky Mountain Chapter, c/o Robert and Sherry Ward, 103 Moss Road, Oak Ridge TN 37830. (615) 482-6857. 128

Texas Home School Coalition, PO Box 6982, Lubbock TX 79493. (806) 797-4927. 11, 137

thisisit, inc., 905 S. Hohokam Drive, Tempe AZ 85281-5115. Toll-free 1-800-555-GROW (4769). 98

Thomas Geale Publications, Inc., PO Box 370540, 483 6th St., Montara CA 94037. FAX (415) 728-0918. Toll-free 1-800-554-5457. 50

Timberdoodle Company, E1510 Spencer Lake Road, Shelton WA 98584. (360) 426-0672. Toll-free ordering 1-800-478-0672. FAX (360) 427-5625. Email: mailbag@timberdoodle.com Internet site: http:/www.timberdoodle.com 50, 59, 73, 93

Tobin's Lab, PO Box 6503, Glendale AZ 85312-6503. (602) 843-4265. Toll-free 1-800-522-4776. Internet site: http://www.primenet.com/~tobinlab 61

TOPS Learning Systems, 10970 S. Mulino Road, Canby OR 97013. FAX (503) 266-5200. 51

Touchphonics Reading Systems, 4900 Birch St., Newport Beach CA 92660. FAX (714) 975-1056. Toll-free 1-800-928-6824. 51

Transparent Language® , 22 Proctor Hill Road, PO Box 575, Hollis NJ 03049.

(603) 465-2230. Toll-free orders 1-800-752-1767. FAX (603) 465-2779. Email: admin@transparent.com 74

Triangle Press, 23 5th Ave. SE, Conrad MT 59425. Phone/ FAX (406) 278-5664. 93

Tri-State Home School Network, PO Box 7193, Newark DE 19714. (302) 368-4217. 123

Trivium Pursuit, 139 Colorado St., Ste 168, Muscatine IA 52761. (309) 537-3641. 93

Unschoolers Network, 2 Smith St., Farmingdale NJ 07727. (908) 938-2473. 126

University of California Extension, Center for Media and Independent Learning, 2000 Center St., Suite 400, Berkeley CA 94704. (510) 642-8245. FAX (510) 643-9271. Email: cmil@ violet.berkeley.edu Internet Site: http://www-cmil.unex.berkeley.ecu/

University of Missouri Center for Independent Study, 136 Clark Hall, Columbis MO 65211. Toll-free 1-800-609-3727. 21, 22

University of Nebraska-Lincoln, Division of Continuing Studies, 269 NCCE, Lincoln NE 68583-9800. (402) 472-4321. FAX (402) 472-1901. Email: unldde@unl.edu Internet site: http://www.unl.edu 22

Usborne Books at Home, 10302 E. 55th Pl., Tulsa OK. (918) 622-4522 Toll-free 1-800-611-1655. 118

Utah Christian Homeschoolers, PO Box 3942, Salt Lake City UT 84110-3942. (801) 969-9657. 129

Utah Home Education Association, 8439 West 3410 South, Magna UT 84044. (801) 252-1011. 129

Vermont Homeschoolers Association, c/o Jim and Mary Smith, RR 1 Box 149, Hartland VT 05048. (802) 436-3146. 129, 137

Vic Lockman, Box 1916, Ramona CA 92065. 94

Video Phonics, 220 Church St., St. Martinville LA 70582. 150

WFF 'N PROOF Learning Games Associates, 1490-FJ South Blvd., Ann Arbor MI 48104-4699. (313) 665-2269. 51, 59, 74

Washington Association of Teaching Christian Homes (WATCH), N. 2904 Dora Road, Spokane WA 99212. 121, 129, 137

Washington Homeschool Organization, 18130 Midvale Ave. N., Seattle WA 98083. 130

Weekly Reader Corporation, 245 Long Hill Road, PO Box 2791, Middletown CT 06457-9291. (860) 638-2400. Customer service toll-free 1-800-446-3355. 84

West Virginia Home Educators Association, (WVHEA), PO Box 3707, Charleston VA 25337-3707. Toll-free 1-800-736-9843 (WVHE). 130

Western Dakota Christian Home Schools (WDCHS), HCR 74, Box 28, Murdo SD 57559. (605) 669-2508. 128, 137

Wildflower Press, 300 Carlsbad Village Dr., Ste. 108A-355, Carlsbad-by-the-Sea CA 92008. Toll-free 1-800-557-5077. 51

Windows to Learning, 8822 Calmada Ave., Whittier CA 90605. (310) 693-3268. FAX (310) 696-9633. Email: wtlearning@aol.com Internet site: http://members.aol.com/wtlearning 52

Wisconsin Christian Home Educators, 2307 Carmel Ave., Racine WI 53405. (414) 637-5127. 130

Wisdom's Gate, PO Box 125, Sawyer MI 49125. 134, 137

Zondervan Directsource, Consumers Order Address: PO Box 668, Holmes PA 19043. 94

Home Schools: An Alternative

4th edition
by Cheryl Gorder

A homeschooling bestseller!
ISBN 0-933025-47-5 $12.95

How has homeschooling evolved from a radical idea into a mainstream movement? Cheryl Gorder explains how. Why is homeschooling better for children psychologically than public schools? Cheryl Gorder explains why. How should a parent get started, if they are interested in homeschooling? Cheryl Gorder shows how.

This homeschooling classic is now in its fourth edition. It has been reviewed over the years by *Library Journal, Booklist, Small Press Book Review, Book Reader, The Family Learing Connection, Home Education Magazine, The Big Book of Home Learning, Parent & Teachers of Gifted Children, Marriage & Family Living*, and many more.

ORDER FORM

To order more books from Blue Bird Publishing, use this handy order form. For a free catalog, write to address below or check Web site: http://www.bluebird1.com

_____*Homeless! Without Addresses in America*	$11.95
_____*Home Schools: An Alternative* (4th edition)	$12.95
_____*Home Education Resource Guide* (4th ed.)	$12.95
_____*Heartful Parenting*	$14.95
_____*Home Business Resource Guide*	$11.95
_____*Dr. Christman's Learn-to-Read Book*	$15.95
_____*Look Inside: Affirmations for Kids*	$18.95
_____*Preschool Learning Activities*	$19.95
_____*Parents' Guide to Helping Kids Become*	
"A" Students	$11.95
_____*Divorced Dad's Handbook*	$12.95
_____*Expanding Your Child's Horizons*	$12.95
_____*Road School*	$14.95
_____*Parent's Guide to a Problem Child*	$11.95
_____*Multicultural Education Resource Guide*	$12.95
_____*Dragon-Slaying for Couples*	$14.95

Shipping Charges: $2.50 for first book. Add 50¢ for each additional book.
Total charges for books: _____
Total shipping charges: _____
TOTAL ENCLOSED: _____

Checks, money orders, and credit cards accepted.
NAME:_____
ADDRESS:_____
CITY, STATE, ZIP:_____

FOR MAIL ORDERS, complete the following:
Please charge my _____VISA _____MasterCard
Card# _____
Expiration Date: _____
Signature: _____
Phone#: _____

BLUE BIRD PUBLISHING
2266 S. Dobson #275
Mesa AZ 85202
(602) 831-6063
FAX (602) 831-1829
E-mail: bluebird@bluebird1.com
Web site: http://www.bluebird1.com